THE MINISTRY OF THE FATHER'S HEART

A JOURNEY OF DISCOVERY

HEATHER THOMPSON

"The Spirit of the Sovereign Lord is on me, because the Lord has anointed me to proclaim good news to the poor. He has sent me to bind up the brokenhearted, to proclaim freedom for the captives and release from darkness for the prisoners."

Isaiah 61:1

Dedication

Dedicated to my daughter Susan, and to my son Niall, daughter-in-law Mags and grandchildren Benjamin, Sophie and Charlotte, each of whom is such joy to me in their unconditional love and encouragement.

May God bless you on your own particular journeys in life.

A JOURNEY OF DISCOVERY

Publisher's statement: Throughout this book, the love for our God is such that whenever we
refer to Him, we honour with capitals. On the other hand, when referring to the devil, we
refuse to acknowledge him with any honour to the point of violating grammatical rule and
withholding capitalisation.

Published by

Maurice Wylie Media
Your Inspirational Christian Publisher

For more information visit
www.MauriceWylieMedia.com

Endorsements

This is the first volume of a series of three books. This introductory volume sets the tone for the series. As I read these opening chapters, I had a very real sense of the presence of God. It was like a spiritual renewal, gaining new insights into the love, grace and provision of God, who loves and cares for His children and wants them to experience life in all its fullness. This is essential reading before coming to the volumes on Deliverance and Healing.

I had the privilege of sharing in many sessions of prayer for healing and deliverance when Heather was ministering to those who were hurt and traumatised by life's experiences. The ministry was gentle, compassionate and loving, with complete reliance on the Lord Jesus Christ, who alone can set the captives free. Many were brought to a new day of freedom, hope and joy.

Rev. T. J. Hagan B.D.
Minister Emeritus,
Donacloney Presbyterian Church, Northern Ireland.

What you are about to read not only reflects the Ministry of the Father's heart of love and compassion for you.... But even more it reflects the depths of Heather's own heart as she has experienced the Father's work in her life and then sought to faithfully, gently, lovingly minister to others over many, many years.

I pray that this book will be an incredible blessing to many as they benefit from Heather's insights and wisdom, gained over years of gentle, sensitive ministry in the power of God's Holy Spirit. So as you read this book, drink in these words of Life and let them lead you to your Heavenly Father. YOU are precious and You are Loved.

Rev. Alvin Little BA BD, (Retired minister)
Shore Street Presbyterian Church, Donaghadee, Northern Ireland.

I know Heather since 2007 and we jokingly referred to each other as 'sparring partners', because we would test and challenge each other's views. As a minister I was keen that Heather would present courses on these topics in our congregation. This she did with much fruit, by God's grace. Her pastoral sensitivity, gracious attitude, love for her Lord, openness to God's Spirit and her fellow Christians, shone through. In these books all of these qualities will be discovered as well. She is a person of integrity and great insight. My prayer is that God would use what she has written to enrich many lives and open their lives for His voice, His loving Father heart and encouraging Spirit.

Annes Nel, Professor at St Petersburg Christian University, BA (Hons - Semitic languages); BA (Hons Psychology); BTh, MTh (Old Testament) and PhD (Systematic Theology).

Contents

Foreword

We all inherit characteristics from our parents. As a child of God, Heather reflects the loving kindness of her heavenly Father and enjoys such a close, intimate relationship with Him. Her overriding passion is to lead people gently to the source of such love in Jesus Christ so that trusting fully in Him, they can become everything that He intends them to be by the power of his indwelling Spirit.

Over the years I have been at the receiving end of Heather's ministry in such powerful ways – the word in season, the timely phone call and the listening ear. Invariably, there is such sensitivity to the prompting of the Holy Spirit, appropriate verses of Scripture, wisdom and insight, discernment and practical advice, support and encouragement. I have always been impressed by her incredible patience and generosity of time and commitment. But then true love never gives up! I think of so many times when I have come to Heather and her ministry team feeling tired and drained, but then after a time of soaking in God's presence, have come away feeling refreshed and renewed.

While so much of Heather's ministry has to do with finding the personal peace and fulfilment of our true identity in Christ, it most definitely does not end there. She is also deeply interested in God's people being blessed and equipped to help, serve and care for others – the Church of Jesus Christ totally alive with all its body parts playing their distinctive role to His praise and glory.

I can't count the number of times over the years I have said to Heather that she must write a book based on so many God-inspired insights, and I am now delighted to be writing a foreword. As I read the ensuing chapters, I felt myself being gently led to a deeper place - slowing down, taking time, absorbing, praying and reflecting. I felt the light of

God's Spirit shining inwardly and bringing illumination to the deepest places of my being. I felt the warm sunshine of God's goodness shining through me, and as I sat at such a beautiful oasis of His stillness, I felt Him speaking to me once more.

Our lives are often at a frantic, frenetic pace and we fill ourselves full of dis-ease, stress and anxiety. Deep down we long for the love, joy and peace of Jesus Christ which alone can slake our thirst and satisfy. Please accept this wonderful invitation to experience the Father heart of God and to discover that you too, are a much-loved child of God. In the words of 1 John 3:1, *"How great is the love the Father has lavished on us, that we should be called children of God."* And that is what we are!

Very Rev. Dr. Charles McMullen
Minister, West Presbyterian Church, Bangor, Northern Ireland.

Introduction

I struggled for a lifetime with fears: fear of man, fear of authority, fear of confrontation and fear of being in the limelight and, despite knowing the truth about who I was in Christ, had not felt secure, relevant or of any worth. Gradually, God has patiently loved and healed me until He was able to reach into the deepest recesses of my heart and flood me with His love, and, as never before, I became free: totally secure, fearless, faith-filled, and dramatically healed, not only from fear but also from chronic back pain of thirty years.

Not only have I received such favour and mercy from my Heavenly Father throughout the years, but I have witnessed many others come into similar freedom and experience healing in its various forms through this ministry of the Father's heart. As I, and others, have learned to listen to and follow God's insights for our own lives and the lives of others, my wonder has grown at the mercy and compassion of our Father for each, at the unfolding of His revelations and wisdom to help in times of need, and at the sheer laughter and enjoyment He shares with His children. He takes delight in each, understanding their hearts, and knowing each intricate path towards freedom, gladly sharing this with those who seek His help.

Many have been set free to enjoy the Father's love and abundant life in Christ. They learned for the first time to hear the Father's voice and enjoy fellowship with Him day by day. Those who were browbeaten and defeated by life circumstances and hurtful relationships were brought into the light and love and freedom of Kingdom living. As each came out of the darkness of their own particular form of slavery and into the light-filled freedom of Jesus, so they, too, have been equipped to go out and lead others into similar freedom. I have been blessed beyond measure, pressed down and running over to such an extent that many times I felt my heart would burst with wonder and joy.

All healing in Jesus' Name, whether we are on the giving or receiving end, takes us closer and closer to our Heavenly Father and deeper and deeper into His love. I pray you will be encouraged as you read, that you will gain insight and understanding as to possible reasons for any present struggle you have, and that, together with the Holy Spirit, you will find your own pathway with God. What is recounted in the three books in the series, The Ministry of the Father's Heart, is not prescriptive but an invitation to explore with God, His specific pathway for you. As you journey with Him, any healing becomes more about the One who is healing than the healing itself, good as it may be. As you enjoy His presence, His Spirit flows freely, bringing freedom, and flows out, blessing others. God bless you as you walk with Him on your journey.

"In Africa, there is a concept known as Ubuntu - the profound sense that we are human only through the humanity of others; that if we are to accomplish anything in this world, it will in equal measure be due to the work and achievement of others," writes Richard Stengel in his portrait of Nelson Mandela.[i]

In essence, we see this in evidence when those who make up the Body of Christ work together harmoniously, each doing its part. In every aspect of my story, others are involved, whether in giving or receiving. More often than not, it is both at the same time. As Scripture says,

"Give, and it will be given to you; good measure, pressed down, shaken together and running over, will be put into your lap. For with the measure you use, it will be measured to you." Luke 6:38

I am who I am because of the many loving, caring and thoughtful people who have been part of my life, many who have nurtured, taught, disciplined, encouraged, supported, helped, believed in and prayed for me and all that concerns me. Some have shouldered burdens willingly and gone the extra mile. Many have shared in the successes and sorrows of the years. I remember all my family members, each important to me beyond words and imprinted on my heart. I recall teachers in school and Sunday School, lecturers, colleagues and students and friends, each leaving a mark on my life. I reflect on my life in West Church, Bangor, and the many who have been and are my church family and special to me. In particular, I thank God for those who have pastored and encouraged me on this road of ministry to the brokenhearted. You each know who you are. As Paul wrote of the Philippians, *"you are my joy and crown."*[1] Thank you to each one of you. May God continue to bless you in your own paths in life.

Clapham Junction is a hive of activity: trains coming in from all directions, emptying commuters at the appropriate platform only to be filled once again with those destined for other places. Clapham Junction would not exist as a railway station without its platforms and trains, and it would neither be useful nor purposeful if there were no commuters. Possibly I should not compare myself to a junction of such note, but there are similarities! I would not have this story were it not for the many areas of ministry in which I have been involved and if there had not been a steady stream of "commuters" passing through my life. I make special mention of those who have journeyed with me in Prayer Ministry[ii] and in the Deeper Ministry,[iii] in Life in the Spirit courses[iv] and in Interflo.[v] Thank you to each of you, my friends, and to all who gave of themselves so freely for others at all sorts of hours in the day and night as we sought God for insight and understanding. We often agonised in the grief and hurt of those seeking freedom, only to burst into laughter at some fun comment from our Father God when He saw that we all needed lifting out of our shared despair. So many times, we laughed until the tears ran down our cheeks. And how great was the overflow of our thanksgiving to our Heavenly Father at every breakthrough. Truly God is amazing in all the diversity that is within His heart of compassion!

---

1 Philippians 4:1.

As I write this first book, one of three in the series, *The Ministry of the Father's Heart*, my prayer is that you experience more and more of the love that God has for you, and that you will become rooted so deeply in His love that you know without doubt that you are uniquely special and have an important place in this world. He wants you to enjoy life with Him and to be free to fulfil all that He plans for you.

Over and over again, God has focussed my attention on Isaiah 61:1-3, indicating His desire that this was the road He wanted me to travel with Him,

> *"The Spirit of the Sovereign Lord is on me, because the Lord has anointed me to proclaim good news to the poor. He has sent me to bind up the broken-hearted, to proclaim freedom for the captives and release from darkness for the prisoners, to proclaim the year of the Lord's favour and the day of vengeance of our God, to comfort all who mourn, and provide for those who grieve in Zion - to bestow on them a crown of beauty instead of ashes, the oil of joy instead of mourning, and a garment of praise instead of a spirit of despair. They will be called oaks of righteousness, a planting of the Lord for the display of his splendour."*

The Ministry of the Father's Heart is a series of three books. This first proclaims the good news that we can have a living relationship with God through Jesus Christ as our Saviour and Lord, the second gives insight into some of the attributes of God with which He gifts us, and reveals ways in which people are released from captivity through knowing the truth in God's Word, and the third gives insights into how God restores those who, because of trauma, have been imprisoned in darkness and are broken-hearted.

First, proclaiming the good news – the ministry of the Father's heart to us all.

SECTION 1

A LOVE THAT REDEEMS US

"Many, Lord my God, are the wonders you have done, the things you planned for us. None can compare with you; were I to speak and tell of your deeds, they would be too many to declare."

Psalms 40:5

Chapter 1:1

God's Will
Wholeness and Fullness for Us

"I have come that they may have life, and that they may have it more abundantly." John 10:10

In the Garden of Eden, Adam and Eve, who had been created in the image and likeness of God, enjoyed full companionship with God, a real and living relationship with Him. There, they lived and communed with Him, free to go anywhere and enjoying everything around them. In His wisdom, God had given them free will, the freedom to make choices for themselves, because he wanted any relationship He had with His created children to be willingly entered into by each. Every day they would walk with Him in the cool of the evening, enjoying fellowship and learning from Him. God had laid down one rule. They could eat from any tree in the garden except one; the tree of knowledge of good and evil. God, Himself, wanted to give them all the knowledge they would need because His knowledge is pure, without prejudice and full of wisdom.

As we know from Scripture, the serpent (satan, the devil) saw his opportunity to break the close relationship that Adam and Eve had with God, and so tempted Eve into breaking God's only rule. He called into question what God had said to Adam,

"Did God really say….?" Genesis 3:1

Eve responded, repeating what God had said. Now, having sown the seeds of doubt into Eve's mind, the serpent continued by refuting what God had said and then adding an enticing invitation, that of having knowledge independently of God and becoming like Him,

> *"You will certainly not die. For God knows that when you eat from it your eyes will be opened, and you will be like God, knowing good and evil."* Genesis 3:4-5

The first statement was a lie, and the second used enticement. The truth was that if they disobeyed God, they would indeed lose their close relationship with God and die spiritually. Despite what the serpent said, they were already like God, although not equal to God, having been made in His image and likeness. We see satan using doubt, then a lie followed by a promise of something they already had, and finally the temptation. We are told in John's epistle that,

> *"Everything in the world - the lust of the flesh, the lust of the eyes, and the pride of life - comes not from the Father but from the world."* 1 John 2:16

While Eve listened to the serpent, her attention was directed towards the forbidden fruit. She saw that it looked inviting,

> *"For everything in the world—the lust of the flesh, the lust of the eyes, and the pride of life—comes not from the Father but from the world. The world and its desires pass away, but whoever does the will of God lives forever."* 1 John 2:16-17

The temptation to eat was great because she could gain knowledge independently of God. We all know what happened. Eve ate from the tree, then told Adam, who also ate from the tree. Their rebellion cost them and their descendants dearly. In choosing to move away from dependence on God, they threw away His gift of friendship with all its benefits. Without the revelation of God the Father to guide them, they no longer had the wisdom of God and began to move down a road of increasing self-destruction. In wanting to please themselves, they had lost what was offered freely.

So began the story of ongoing rebellion against God by the very ones He has created, but, despite this rebellion, God still wants to enjoy a true relationship with His children. He knew from the beginning of time that we would choose the path of independence and self-destruction if given the freedom to do so, but so great is His love for all He created that He provided the solution. Man's sin would lead to certain death and separation from God because sin cannot come near a holy God. Only by providing a way out from this separation could God and man be reunited forever.

Throughout this book, you will read of many wonders orchestrated by God our heavenly Father; how He has provided a way for each of us to be restored into a close relationship with Him despite our sin, and how He releases wonders and miracles, setting free those who are captive in spirit, soul and body. You will witness His deep compassionate love for every person, no matter what they feel or think about themselves. As we spent time in His presence, He revealed His deep understanding of all who were hurting and fearful, and, with His insight, mercy, and love, He led each through their labyrinth of pain and rejection and out into healing. This is one aspect of the ongoing salvation that Paul talks about throughout His epistles. In his letter to the Philippian Church, he has this to say,

"Therefore, my beloved, as you have always obeyed, not as in my presence only, but now much more in my absence, work out your own salvation with fear and trembling; for it is God who works in you both to will and to do for His good pleasure." Philippians 2:12-13

Once we receive Jesus into our lives and journey with Him in humility and respect, honouring Him as Lord, we can each move towards new freedoms, a process of receiving wholeness and fullness in Christ. This embraces all healing of the spirit, the soul and the body.

When I asked God what He wanted us to call this ministry to the broken-hearted, His response was, "The Heart of the Father Ministering to the Lost and Needy." It has been, and continues to be, a journey into the depths of the Father's heart of love, made possible because Jesus has taken the curse of sin and provided the way for our redemption, and the Spirit of God and of Jesus helps us by remaining with us, giving insights and guiding us.

The understanding of brokenness, and of the truths that have been revealed, are true for all, Christian and non-Christian alike, but only those who have asked Jesus into their lives and who are willing to let Jesus lead them are able to journey along this road to wholeness for it is a road travelled in the company of our Heavenly Father, and by the power of the Holy Spirit. The Scripture that God gave us to describe the ministry is this,

> *"His [God's] intent was that now, through the church, the manifold wisdom of God should be known to the rulers and authorities in the Heavenly realm according to His eternal purpose which He accomplished in Christ Jesus our Lord."* Ephesians 3:10-11

In these verses, we read that God has chosen to use the Church through which to reveal His wisdom to accomplish what He has ordained, while undoing the work of the enemy, devious and evil as it is. He calls us to put off the practices of the old man and to put on the new self who is being renewed,[2] to take every thought captive in obedience to Christ

---

2 Colossians 3:3-15.

and to be renewed in the spirit of our minds.[3] As we minister in the Name of Jesus and witness the wonder of His love and understanding for those damaged by, or caught up in, perversion and evil, we find ourselves worshipping and longing to be closer to the Living God. He alone is the One who can pull down and rebuild. It is through Him in His wisdom that,

> *"A house is built, and through understanding it is established; through knowledge its rooms are filled with rare and beautiful treasures."*
> Proverbs 24:3-4

As we bear witness to His love in action we find ourselves hungry to know Him better. We stand enthralled at this God of love and bow before Him, giving Him all honour and glory,

> *"Surely our God is the God of gods, the Lord of kings, the Revealer of mysteries...."*[vi 4]

Over the years, this story has been and continues to be God's story. Step by step He has drawn back the curtains of our ignorance and revealed the hidden secrets. He has guided us as we have been available to help those who are downcast and who struggle with life. He has given us knowledge and wisdom so that, in Jesus' Name, we could bring freedom to the captives and sight to the spiritually blind. It is all God's doing. Right from the outset, I want to make it clear that all the healing that has taken place through *The Ministry of the Father's Heart* in people's lives is because of His love for them and their response to that love.

We began our journey in this ministry thirty years ago. Love and compassion for the broken-hearted drew us into wanting to help them.

---

3 Ephesians 4:23.
4 Daniel 2:47.

We knew nothing and felt totally inadequate, but that meant that we depended on God to give us insight and understanding at each step. Over the years, I have come to understand what God meant when He told me some five years earlier that I would be "a counsellor of patience". This is a ministry that requires not only patience, but diligence, perseverance and forbearance in love, all graces given by God. It is also a ministry that reveals mysteries and, above all, the heart of the Father.

On our journey, we were shown that there are different ways in which trauma may affect a person, each with its own specific symptoms and path to resolution. All that will be described here is neither comprehensive nor does it highlight the only routes to healing. It is merely a snapshot of how we were led, and through describing it, I hope that, with the help of the Holy Spirit, many will find their own route to abundant life in Jesus.

We can consider the spiritual, the emotional and the physical. Because these three are closely interlinked in man, each has an impact on the others. For example, a diagnosis of cancer (physical) can lead to feelings of despair (emotional) and possibly anger at and perceived rejection by God (spiritual). A crushed spirit (spiritual) dries up the bones (physical).[5] Complete releasing from any symptom often requires healing in more than one aspect of life. Within this series of three books, we will consider seven aspects of healing:

- o   Spiritual Healing
- o   Inner Healing or Healing from Past Hurts
- o   Physical Healing
- o   Restoration of the Attributes of the Spirit to Greater Fullness
- o   Deliverance from Evil Spirits
- o   Healing from Fragmenting of the Personality
- o   Healing of the Heart.

---

5 Proverbs 17: 22.

This first book discusses Spiritual Healing, Inner Healing and Physical Healing, the second, Deliverance from Evil Spirits and Restoration of the Attributes of the Spirit to Greater Fullness, and the third, Healing from Fragmentation of the Personality and Healing of the Heart.

So as to have clarity in gaining insights into healing we will consider each of these in turn, but, in practice, any healing within a person may include any one, some, or all of these. The book of Proverbs has much to offer by way of advice,

"The fear of the Lord is a fountain of life, turning a man from the snares of death." Proverbs 14:27

"The fear of the Lord is the beginning of wisdom and knowledge of the Holy One is understanding." Proverbs 9:10

"The heart of the discerning acquires knowledge; the ears of the wise seek it out." Proverbs 18:15

"Apply your hearts to instruction and your ears to words of knowledge." Proverbs 23:12

"A wise man has great power, and a man of knowledge increases strength; for waging war you need guidance, and for victory many advisors." Proverbs 24:5-6

It is a wonderful journey. Enjoy it with our Father God.

Chapter 1:2

Our Father Loves Us

"Look with wonder at the depth of the Father's marvellous love that he has lavished on us! He has called us and made us his very own beloved children." 1 John 3:1 TPT

From eternity God had prepared the way for His solution to the sin separation that He knew would occur between Him and His created children. He chose a people group, the Israelites, through whom He would reveal Himself to the world. He taught these people His ways and sent messengers to instruct them and foretell His great plan of redemption. He gave foretastes of what was to come by empowering prophets, priests and kings with His Spirit to do the work they were called to do.

Throughout history, He unfolded more and more of His character, revealing this one step at a time...

The Lord our righteousness -**Yahweh Tsidkenuh** Jeremiah 23:6
The Lord who sanctifies -**Yahweh M'Kaddesh** Leviticus 29:7-8
The Lord our Peace -**Yahweh Shalom** Judges 6:24
The Lord who is there -**Yahweh Shammah** Ezekiel 48:35
The Lord our Provider -**Yahweh Yireh** Genesis 22:14
The Lord our Shepherd -**Yahweh Rohi** Psalm 23

The Lord my Banner -**Yahweh Nissi** Exodus 17:15
The Lord our Healer -**Yahweh Rophe** Exodus 15:26

Over centuries He repeatedly demonstrated His forgiveness and patience to His rebellious people, ordinary people like you and me.

Love is the personality of God. Anyone who meets with God meets with love. Whoever abides in God abides in love.[6] The love of God is a mystery because it doesn't make sense. It is supernatural and far above and beyond reason.[7] It is a mystery to satan and hid God's plan of redemption through the death and resurrection of Jesus.[8] God loves us just because He loves us, no matter what we've done,

"The Lord appeared to us in the past, saying: 'I have loved you with an everlasting love; I have drawn you with unfailing kindness."
Jeremiah 31:3

His love cannot be earned or deserved and reveals the hope that we have.[9] It is neither a love borne out of attraction ("érōs") nor a love as found in a family ("storgē"), nor the love that is shared amongst friends, emotional love ("phileō"). These loves are often conditional, may be fickle, and are not always birthed of God.

God's love is much more than any of these. It is a love that is volitional, unconditional, faithful, impartial and eternal ("agápé").

God longs to enter into the hearts of men and women with His love, but so often there are obstacles such as valleys of pain and hurt, mountains of unbelief and doubt, crooked places of criticism and fear within us. These obstacles can arise through life experiences and a wrong perception of who God is; and because of misguided thinking about how He relates

---

6 John 15:4-9; 1 John 4:16.
7 1 Corinthians 1:18.
8 1 Corinthians 2:7-8.
9 Romans 5:5.

to us. We can transfer our own experience of human relationships and of life events onto God and see Him through a distorted lens. We may even see God through the eyes of our own attainment rather than relate to Him in a way that is based on His heart. In the Book of Jeremiah, we read,

> *"Let not the wise man glory in His wisdom, nor let the mighty man glory in his might, nor let the rich man glory in his riches [don't come to Him on the basis of our own achievements---my paraphrase]; but let him who glories glory in this, that He understands and knows Me, that I am the Lord, exercising loving-kindness, judgment, and righteousness in the earth. For in these I delight, says the Lord."*
> Jeremiah 9:23-24

Let our first focus be on getting to know the heart of God our Father. Knowing our Heavenly Father, knowing His heart, helps us discover who we truly are and empowers us to help others out of their misery and into the embrace of Father God. Through God's healing, the crooked places in our hearts become straightened out, the insensitivities and irrationalities of our attitudes dispersed, the dry places watered, and the hunger satisfied. As we live a life of abiding in Christ and in His Word, we can come to know the heart of God our Father and experience His amazing love for us. Our preconceptions about how He thinks of us may initially be formed more by our experiences of life than by our experience of Him, but as we get to know Him and His ways through opening up more and more of our hearts to Him, we find the true heart of God and are enabled to welcome His presence into our own lives and the life of the Church. The more we live with and abide in Him, the more He is free to show us His heart and to live through us, and what can begin as head knowledge that God loves me can become our deeply known experience. Our Father says,

> *"Behold, I will do a new thing, Now, it shall spring forth: Shall you not know it? I will even make a road in the wilderness and rivers in*

*the desert. The beast of the field will honour me, the jackals and the
ostriches, Because I give waters in the wilderness and rivers in the
desert, To give drink to My people, My chosen. This people I have
formed for Myself."* Isaiah 43:19

Isaiah is speaking of a time in the future, both physically and spiritually.
God will cause rivers to flow through the deserts in our hearts, waters to
flow through the wildernesses, and as He does this our lives will overflow
with His fullness, the Church will be filled with His Spirit, and God
will manifest His presence even more amongst us.

Although we can feel helpless in this world of so much evil and feel
oppressed by it at times, and although we can feel helpless in the face of
other people's personal calamities, we can remember that we are children
of a loving Father, called to share His love with others. As we minister
in His Name we can do so with confidence because He is love, love that
conquers all and that is stronger than death. He is the light dispersing
darkness, the healer of hearts and the binder of wounds. He is the one
who sets the captives free. As we wait before our Father, we receive hope
that He can change things, bright hope for ourselves and for others.

At the centre is the love of God our Father for each one of us. The
Holy Spirit breathes His life through the words of Scripture as we read
and so we come to know who God is, what He is really like, and how
much He watches out for us. Then, as we relate to Him, we come to
know His expansive heart of love that continuously embraces us. The
more we receive His love, the more we love in return, and the stronger
love becomes within us for others. If we do not live in our relationship
to Him on the basis of scriptural truth, then everything else that we
focus on will become distorted. We may find it easy to acknowledge
His true character when things are going well for us, but, sometimes,
when problems arise and situations disturb us and we don't seem to
find a way through, we may feel that we don't really know Him, or
question whether He is really there for us when we most need Him. In

the difficult times we might even question whether He really does love us but in those times we do well to acknowledge to Him how we really feel but at the same time hold on to the truth about what Scripture says about His true character. Our experiences do not determine who God is because they can be absolutely brilliant at times and then completely crash at others. God is consistent, faithful, and unconditional in His love and so we need never fear that He will ever leave us. When we are confident in these truths about God, we are strengthened and are able to strengthen those who are struggling or wavering. As we grow in love for God, we find ourselves gazing upon Him, beholding Him and moving into worship.

For Reflection
In 1 Samuel 13:14, think about how God related to King David, *"a man after God's own heart."* What do you think this phrase means? We know that Jesus equated obedience with love[10] and that David was sincerely devoted to following God's commands, but we also know that he was far from being a model of obedience. Did God still think of him as *"a man after God's own heart"* after his adultery and murder? Read Acts 13:22 to see what Paul was inspired to write a thousand years after David had died. Why do you think that God said that in the face of David's weaknesses? What do you think was the key in David's life? Perhaps it was that David was able to see the heart of God for him. We know from the Psalms that he spent time with God not only praising Him but pouring out his pain to the God whom he knew still loved him in his down times. As he focussed on God and away from his turmoil, he readily moved into worship and regained his confidence.

While on earth, Jesus revealed the Father heart of God. And now, in these days, the Holy Spirit is willing to give us revelation about the heart of God as we seek to know Him. It is easier for us to open up to God when we know that He loves us as we are no longer guarded because of fear. Does it make a difference to you knowing that God really knows

---

10 John 14:23.

your heart and doesn't look on you as a hypocrite and reject you, but that He understands your weakness and loves you unconditionally? Our intentions to obey are very significant to God. He notices our desires, not just our outward actions. It might be helpful to you to pause here and reflect on how you have experienced the heart of God in your down times? Allow this to lead you into worshipping God from your heart.

As the God who loves us unconditionally, He wants us to share in that same relationship that He enjoys within Himself, Father Son and Holy Spirit. For this to happen we must be free to choose to do so or not but, as we read in the history of God's relationship with His people, we see that they often rebelled against the One who had created them. Over and over again God rescued them and forgave them only to have them turn their backs on Him once again. As we said previously, God's solution was the ultimate in self-denial, coming to earth as a man,

"Who, being in very nature God, did not consider equality with God something to be used to his own advantage; rather, he made himself nothing by taking the very nature of a servant, being made in human likeness. And being found in appearance as a man, he humbled himself by becoming obedient to death - even death on a cross!" Philippians 2: 6-8

"But God demonstrates his own love for us in this: while we were still sinners, Christ died for us." Romans 5:8

As a man, Jesus confirmed and revealed much more about the unfailing, unconditional, and unmerited love and favour of God. His life was marked by compassion, by unconditional and unbiased love ("agápé"), by mercy, grace and forgiveness. He demonstrated true righteousness and justice, teaching the need to treat others as ourselves, to be fair and considerate of the welfare of others. He revealed that He was the Way, the Truth and the Life and that there was no other way to God than through Him.

Chapter 1:3

Why Jesus and the Cross?

"And the Word became flesh and dwelt among us, and we beheld His glory, the glory as of the only begotten of the Father, full of grace and truth." John 1:14

Under the Old Covenant, God had made it clear to His people that, because of their sin, they could not approach Him because He is a holy God and His holiness would consume them and lead to their death. He taught that the punishment for sin is death and that the only way God could restore His people into close relationship with Him was through the shedding of blood on their behalf. Under the Old Covenant, this was achieved through the substitutionary sacrifice of animals which pointed forward to the once-for-all sacrificial death of Jesus Christ.

Throughout history, God had spoken through the prophets telling of a time when a sin-bearing Saviour would come to earth[11] so that all could be restored in their relationship with God. The appointed time came when Jesus, Son of God, came to earth in human form to reveal more of the Father heart of God by demonstrating God's mercy through His compassion, through healing from sicknesses and diseases, and through deliverance from evil spirits of torment. He taught what the Kingdom of Heaven is like and demonstrated to His listeners a new way of living and relationship with God. He spoke against practising a form of religion

---

11 Isaiah 52,53 and many other Scriptures.

while neglecting a relationship with God, and, in living a sin-free life, He demonstrated how life could be lived through the grace of God. Throughout this time, He discipled twelve men in preparation for the next phase, which was to come after He had completed His earthly mission.

The religious leaders of the time turned against Him and His teaching and plotted to find a way of accusing Him and having Him put to death. Despite having lived a life free from sin, He was condemned to death on a cross. He had made it clear to His followers that no-one could take His life even though it might look that way, but that He was laying His life down for the sake of all whom God had created so that they could have the choice of returning to a close relationship with Him. He voluntarily took upon Himself all the sin and sicknesses of mankind, together with the wrath and anger of God at sin, and bore it all as He died on the cross so that sin would not separate us from God when we depart this life.

Since Jesus was blameless, death could not hold him, and so, in rising from the dead, He overcame every evil and sin that could separate us from enjoying the love of God. Now, those who choose to turn away from sin, believing that Jesus took their sins and the punishment for them when He died on the cross, can invite Him to enter into their lives and be made new. In receiving and responding to this truth, we acknowledge that we were buried with Christ and rose to new life in Him at His resurrection. This is what is meant by being born again to a new and different life in Christ. Jesus describes to Nicodemus how this transformation could take place,

"Jesus answered and said to him, 'Most assuredly, I say to you, unless one is born again, he cannot see the kingdom of God.' " John 3:3

Jesus then goes on to challenge what Nicodemus believed. Being a religious person, living with religious people and obeying religious laws would not save him. Jesus was teaching that nothing we do can save us from death, but only what God will do to create us anew. He was talking about a spiritual mystery which cannot be understood with our reasoning. In order to help Nicodemus to understand, Jesus took the familiar to lead into a spiritual understanding of the unfamiliar,

> *"Most assuredly, I say to you, unless one is born of water and the Spirit, he cannot enter the kingdom of God. That which is born of the flesh is flesh, and that which is born of the Spirit is spirit. Do not marvel that I said to you, 'You must be born again. The wind blows where it wishes, and you hear the sound of it, but cannot tell where it comes from and where it goes. So is everyone who is born of the Spirit.'"* John 3:5-8

This process of acknowledging our sin and choosing to turn away from it, is called repentance in the Bible. John Roberts[vii] explains the change in this way:

"The New Testament Greek word translated as 'repent' is METANOEO. It has two parts: META and NOEO. The second part, NOEO, refers to the disposition of your inner self, your 'default setting' toward reality. The first part, META, is a prefix that means movement or change. META, or 'change,' plus NOEO, or 'disposition' equals 'to change your disposition towards life and reality, to have a transformed default setting about what's important."

While calling his listeners to repentance, Peter explained what change they could expect,

> *"And now you must repent and turn back to God so that your sins will be removed, and so that times of refreshing will stream from the Lord's presence.'"* Acts 3:19 TPT

Once we recognise our own sinfulness and our need for help in overcoming it, the Spirit of God enables us to respond to the new way of living that Jesus offers us,

"For by grace you have been saved by faith. Nothing you did could ever earn this salvation, for it was the love gift from God that brought us to Christ! So no one will ever be able to boast, for salvation is never a reward for good works or human striving." Ephesians 2:8-9 TPT

Notice that Paul tells us that nothing we do can ever earn us our salvation. We receive this gift through grace by faith. Grace is the unmerited favour of God. It is His ability given to us freely. Faith is also a gift of God and is belief and trust in what Jesus did for us on the cross.

When, through the quickening of the Holy Spirit the depths of this truth penetrate beyond mere cerebral assent into our hearts, we become convicted of our sin. As we acknowledge our need of the Saviour and invite Him into our lives to help us, He comes by His Spirit, and life bursts forth from within and the burdens and heaviness of years disappear. For the first time, we experience total freedom exploding from the core of our being. We are truly, "born again" as we have become new creations.[12] From that moment on, we are instantly in right standing with God because,

"God made him who had no sin to be sin for us, so that in him we might become the righteousness of God." 2 Corinthians 5:21

In Christ, we are righteous and that is how God sees us. If you would like to invite Jesus to be your Saviour and Lord, you could pause from reading and talk to Him about this now. He loves you and is waiting for your invitation.

---

12 2 Corinthians 5:17.

Once we have invited Him into our lives, we enter into eternal life in Christ, a life that never ends. Just as Jesus explained to Nicodemus, our spirits are re-born with the life of the Spirit; we are given a new nature, and our souls and bodies begin a life of transformation under the leading of the Holy Spirit, bringing us into alignment with our new nature. Each of us is spirit, has a soul and lives in a body. Our spirit is who we are, and now that it has been renewed it is righteous because the Spirit of Jesus dwells within. Any sinful thoughts, attitudes or actions that we have from this time on are coming from our souls and bodies, which as yet have still to undergo progressive change into alignment with the Spirit of Jesus within us. God taught through the prophets, that this transformation would take place because His people would be given a new heart and a new spirit,

> *"I will give you a new heart and put a new spirit in you; I will remove from you your heart of stone and give you a heart of flesh. And I will put my Spirit in you and move you to follow my decrees and be careful to keep my laws."* Ezekiel 36:26-27

It was to be a time when each of us could come to know the Lord for ourselves,

> *"This is the covenant I will make with the people of Israel after that time,"* declares the Lord. *"I will put my law in their minds and write it on their hearts. I will be their God, and they will be my people. No longer will they teach their neighbour, or say to one another, 'Know the Lord,' because they will all know me, from the least of them to the greatest,'"* declares the Lord. *"For I will forgive their wickedness and will remember their sins no more."* Jeremiah 31:33-34

…and know Him as our Shepherd and Protector,

> *"I will tend them in a good pasture, and the mountain heights of Israel will be their grazing land. There they will lie down in*

good grazing land, and there they will feed in a rich pasture on the mountains of Israel. I myself will tend my sheep and have them lie down, declares the Sovereign Lord." Ezekiel 34:14-15

When our physical bodies die our spirit and soul goes to live with Him,

"For God so loved the world that he gave his one and only Son, that whoever believes in him shall not perish but have eternal life. For God did not send his Son into the world to condemn the world, but to save the world through him. Whoever believes in him is not condemned, but whoever does not believe stands condemned already because they have not believed in the name of God's one and only Son." John 3:16-18

"But as many as received Him, to them He gave the right to become children of God, to those who believe in His name." John 1:12

Throughout our lives, the Holy Spirit continues to help us as we turn from sin and change our ways, and as Jesus cleanses us from sin and its effects upon us. As we come to Him willing to forgive others who have done us wrong, He releases us from the impact of sin against us and heals our hearts. Gradually, step by step, He heals and delivers us from the effects of sin on our lives, whether it be inherited, personal, or caused by someone else. His desire is that we live our lives in Christ here on earth as free as possible. Paul writes,

"Shall we go on sinning so that grace may increase? Certainly not! How shall we who died to sin live any longer in it? Or do you not know that as many of us as were baptised into Christ Jesus were baptised into His death? Therefore, we were buried with Him through baptism into death, that just as Christ was raised from the dead by the glory of the Father, even so we also should walk in newness of life. For if we have been united together in the likeness of His death, certainly we also shall be in the likeness of His resurrection, knowing

this, that our old man was crucified with Him, that the body of sin might be done away with, that we should no longer be slaves of sin. For he who has died has been freed from sin. Now if we died with Christ, we believe that we shall also live with Him, knowing that Christ, having been raised from the dead, dies no more. Death no longer has dominion over Him. For the death that He died, He died to sin once for all; but the life that He lives, He lives to God. Likewise, you also, reckon yourselves to be dead indeed to sin, but alive to God in Christ Jesus our Lord." Romans 6:1-11 NKJV

We will talk about this process of transformation in our lives throughout later chapters; change that would never take place were it not for the cross.

Some people in our churches have not fully understood that when they gave their lives to Jesus, they were only at the beginning of a journey to complete wholeness in Him. They think that as Christians, they should instantly be perfect and free from all sinful attitudes and behaviours. Yes, it is true that when we invite Jesus Christ into our hearts to reign, a change takes place, and we are transferred out of the dominion of darkness and into the Kingdom of the Beloved Son, Jesus.[13] Our spirits are immediately transformed, but our souls are not. We are at the beginning of a life-long process during which we learn more and more about the love of the Father, the saving grace of the Lord Jesus, and the empowerment of the Holy Spirit, a process that releases us from the bondages of "the world, the flesh and the devil", and that draws us closer in communion with our Lord. There is no quick fix,

> *"...they have healed the brokenness of my people superficially, saying, 'Peace, peace,' but there is no peace."* Jeremiah 6:14

Sadly, many of us struggle against thoughts that violate our sense of propriety, intrusive, unpleasant and sinful thoughts. We may fight

---

13 Colossians 1:13.

internally against dark passions and feel driven in an inexplicable way towards evil actions that seem to take us ruthlessly in a downwards spiral of self-destruction and the destruction of others. Even those who profess Jesus Christ as Lord and Saviour may be subject to an inner tyranny that plagues them and causes them to cry from the inner heart for help. And yet they remain silent, struggling to put on a good face, trying to subdue what they do not like about themselves and feeling horribly guilty, miserable, and useless as Christians. A common cry might be, "I can't be a Christian!" or "I shouldn't think like this as a Christian!" Sometimes impatient with themselves, they may exclaim, "I shouldn't be feeling like this - I have no reason to!" Many are too frightened to admit they are struggling in case they are criticized. Many are fearful that they will get quoted at by someone who apparently lives victoriously in Christ so they keep their heads down and live a life of pretence, a non-abundant life. Why does the Church sometimes fall short of being the healing, nurturing body of Christ? Perhaps it is because of a lack of insight or understanding about the process of sanctification,

"Where there is no vision the people perish." Proverbs 29:18

We all need wisdom and insight of God. Paul writes,

"My conscience is clear, but that does not make me innocent. It is the Lord who judges me. Therefore, judge nothing before the appointed time; wait till the Lord comes. He will bring to light what is hidden in darkness and will expose the motives of men's hearts. At that time each will receive his praise from God." 1 Corinthians 4:4-5

Hidden things within can often block us in our Christian walk and keep us from being one with God and with each other. No matter how hard we try, we sometimes cannot overcome the negativity and judgementalism that divides. Any healing needs to go deep to the root of any problem. That journey of exploration needs the guidance of the Father who loves us, knows all about us, and who can set us free through the power of His Spirit because of what Jesus did for us at the cross. He removes hurt and pain, drawing us into healthy thinking and attitudes and uncovers,

"The treasures of the darkness, riches stored in the secret places."
Isaiah 45:3a

This treasure is the beauty within each of us that has become hidden by the sinfulness of human nature. Such restoration enables us to have greater freedom in knowing the living God in ever-increasing measure and in knowing that He knows us and deeply loves us. He is,

"The Lord, the God of Israel who summons you by name." Isaiah 43:3b

We know that our first love and focus need to be on God, on who He is and on our relationship with Him through Jesus, His Son. Worship is at the heart of welcoming Jesus among us. Worship is at the heart of making the change in our lives a reality. Worship enables the changes that make the roads smooth and prepare the way for the Lord.

Paul taught that throughout our lives, we should go on being filled with the Spirit,

".... but be filled [and keep on being filled] with the [Holy] Spirit and constantly guided by Him." Ephesians 5:18

Jackie Pullinger[viii] is well known for her work amongst drug addicts in Hong Kong. At one time, she held a clinic on a Wednesday to which former drug addicts, now Christians, invited their unsaved friends. "Come and meet Jesus," they would say. Jackie quickly discovered that drug addicts could not focus or settle sufficiently to listen to the Gospel message and eventually realised that after she had invited the Holy Spirit to come and rest on the drug addicts, they would begin to feel peace, something they had not known before. At this point, Jackie knew that they would be receptive to the message of freedom that she had for them because the Holy Spirit was opening the eyes of their understanding as they listened to her explain the gospel,

> *"And we articulate these realities with the words imparted to us by the Spirit and not with the words taught by human wisdom. We join together Spirit-revealed truths with Spirit-revealed words. Someone living on an entirely human level rejects the revelations of God's Spirit, for they make no sense to him. He can't understand the revelations of the Spirit because they are only discovered by the illumination of the Spirit."* 1 Corinthians 2:13-16 TPT

As we yield more and more of our lives to Jesus as Lord, we can open ourselves more and more to Him, inviting Him to keep filling us with His Spirit so that we are immersed and empowered by the Spirit of Jesus. The Spirit within us releases the power and authority of Jesus and His gifts of grace to build up and heal us personally and corporately, and to reach out to unbelievers. As we walk in the Spirit, we bring in God's Kingdom with love and power, a Kingdom which "is not a matter of talk but of power".[14] The battle we have is a battle against spiritual forces and authorities in high places, and so the weapons with which we fight are not the methods of the world but spiritually sourced. It is only the Spirit of God within us who enables us to overcome. The question then arises in our minds, "What do we know about the Spirit of God?" We will now discuss this.

---

14 1 Corinthians 4:20.

God in us, The Holy Spirit

---

*"If you love Me, keep My commandments. And I will pray the Father,
and He will give you another Helper, that He may abide with you
forever— the Spirit of truth."* John 14:15-16

Many people are puzzled when Christians talk about the Holy Spirit.
They may understand what we mean when we talk about God the
Father, or about Jesus the Son of God, but when we mention the Holy
Spirit, they are often bewildered. Some Christians, too, are uncertain
where He fits in and what His role is. Before I discuss the scriptural
references describing who the Holy Spirit is and what He is like, it is
important that I say, above all, that He is my friend, my helper and my
confidant. He teaches me about Jesus, causing my spirit to become alive
in worship, and alerts me when I am off track in my journey with Jesus.
He guides me, warns me, and reveals what my Father wants me to know.

The Holy Spirit is the Spirit of Jesus and of God. He is the third part
of the Trinity,[15] co-equal with God the Father and Jesus His Son. He is
always present so I can seek His wisdom at all times.[16] Together they are
one: God the Father, Jesus the Son, and the Holy Spirit, a circle of love
inviting each of us into that circle to enjoy fellowship with the triune
God. His presence is associated with sharing the Good News about

---

15 Matthew 28:19, 2 Corinthians 1:3-4, 1 Peter 1:2.
16 Psalm 139:7-10.

Jesus as He is the one who brings an understanding of the sacrifice that Jesus paid on the cross for each of us.

He loves us[17] and wants to help us so that we can have peace within ourselves, peace with others and peace with God. Through the grace of God, He helps us to change our thoughts, attitudes and actions, so that we can fellowship unhindered with the God the Father, Son and Holy Spirit.[18]

In the Old Testament, He is described as being active in creation.[19] He is portrayed as wind and as the breath that gives Life;[20] as water, symbolising spiritual refreshment, cleansing and blessing;[21] as fire, symbolising cleansing and refining;[22] as oil, used in anointing kings and priests for God's service and symbolising the equipping for service with the necessary resources of God's Spirit;[23] and as a dove, symbolising being a messenger from God.[24]

In the New Testament, we read that He was present in power at the conception of Jesus, and that He gave revelation about the coming of a Saviour to Simeon, prompting him to be at the temple when Jesus was brought to be circumcised.[25] When Jesus was baptised, He came in the likeness of a dove to confirm that this was the promised Messiah.[26] He led Jesus into the desert and, in response to Jesus' obedience and overcoming of temptation, He empowered Him for the work that lay ahead.[27] As Jesus preached and did signs and wonders, it was in partnership with the Holy Spirit.[28] Before Jesus left the earth, He told

17 Romans 15:30.
18 Psalm 51:11; John 16:8-1
19 Genesis 1:1; Psalm 104:30.
20 Exodus 10:13; 14: 21; Ezekiel 37:1-14.
21 Ezekiel 47:1-12, Jeremiah 2:13, 17:13.
22 Exodus 3:2, 13:21; Isaiah 66:1
23 Exodus 30:22ff; 1 Samuel 16:13; Isaiah 61:1; Zechariah 4:1-3.
24 Genesis 8:1-12.
25 Luke 1:35, 2:25-32.
26 Luke 3:16.
27 Luke 4:1,14.
28 Matthew 12:28.

His disciples,

"Lo, I am with you always even to the end of the age." Matthew 28:20

He explained to His disciples that this promise would be fulfilled by "another like Him," the Holy Spirit,[29] the One who would point us all to Jesus and give all glory to Him.

We might think that the disciples who had lived with Jesus for three years and had healed the sick and cast out demons were adequately equipped to witness, but they were not. In addition to their experience, training and knowledge, they needed divine power. This power would be the Holy Spirit, whom Jesus and God the Father would send upon them after He had ascended to the right hand of His Father,

"I am going to send you what my Father has promised; but stay in the city until you have been clothed with power from on high." Luke 24:49

Jesus told the disciples that this would equip them with power to witness,

"But you will receive power when the Holy Spirit comes on you; and you will be my witnesses in Jerusalem, and in all Judea and Samaria, and to the ends of the earth." Acts 1:8

In Acts 2, we read that, at Pentecost, while the disciples were waiting in the Upper Room in Jerusalem, the Holy Spirit came down upon them. This outpouring is described as the blowing of wind and tongues of fire and led to empowered preaching, conviction of sin, amazing signs and wonders, and to the birth of the Church. Since then, all who have received Jesus as Saviour and Lord are born again, become part of the body of Christ, the Christian community, and the Church

---

29 John 14:15-27; 15:26; 16:5-15.

worldwide. Like the disciples, we are encouraged to spend time with God regularly and invite the Holy Spirit to keep filling us and equipping us for whatever we do in Jesus' name.

He is the Spirit of truth, who hears us, speaks to us and intercedes for us. He is our teacher and counsellor who guides us into truth by giving us spiritual insight and wisdom from God, by helping us to understand what we are reading in the Scriptures and revealing Jesus through them, and by telling us what the Father wants us to know.[30] His desire is to glorify Jesus by leading us into worship in spirit and truth, and He fosters our relationship with God. As we pray, the Holy Spirit leads us in how to pray, and, as we live closely with Jesus, the Holy Spirit works gently in our lives, developing fruit,

"But the fruit of the Spirit is love, joy, peace, forbearance, kindness, goodness, faithfulness, gentleness and self-control. Against such things there is no law." Galatians 5:22-23

He is grieved when people rebel against God,[31] and is gentle, never drawing attention to Himself, and easily quenched if we do not allow Him freedom.

He releases His gifts within each believer to build up and empower the Church and to equip us for witness through preaching, teaching, healing and deliverance.[32] He also equips people with the skills necessary for their work,[33] and gives specific guidance.[34] He is the Spirit of Prophecy.[35]

There are many testimonies to the supernatural empowering of the Holy Spirit in many different aspects of life threaded throughout Scripture.[36]

---

30 John 14:15-17, 26; 16:7; Romans 8:26; 1 Corinthians 2:7-13.
31 Isaiah 63:10.
32 1 Corinthians 12:7-11.
33 Exodus 31:1-4.
34 Isaiah 63:11ff; Acts 16:6-10.
35 Ezekiel 37; Micah 3: 8, 1 Kings 22:24; Ephesians 3:2-5.
36 Acts 4:33, and 6:8; 10:38, Romans 15:13-19, 1 Corinthians 2:4-5, 2 Corinthians 6:6-10, 10:4-6, 12:9, Ephesians 3:16, 6:10, Philippians 4:13, 1 Thessalonians 1:5, and 2 Timothy 1:7, 3:4-5.

Through the presence of the Holy Spirit, we are transformed, given boldness, and strengthened to endure hardship and persecution.[37] And as we walk in dependence on Jesus, seeking His face, obeying and overcoming temptation, the Holy Spirit empowers us for witness.[38] When we come to Jesus and ask to be baptised or filled with His Spirit, we don't come on the basis of our own efforts but on the basis of His offer of grace. He invites anyone who is thirsty for Him to come to Him and be filled with His Living Water,

"If anyone is thirsty, let him come to Me and drink. Whoever believes in Me, as the Scripture has said, streams of living water will flow from within him. By this He meant the Spirit, whom those who believed in Him were later to receive." John 7:37-38

As John and Matthew tell us, Jesus, and only Jesus, is the One who baptises in the Holy Spirit and with fire.[39] [40]

We are called to be witnesses to Jesus and what He has done for us in reconciling us to God both through our lifestyles and how we serve others. Our primary witness arises out of our relationship with Jesus, and anything we do will only be fruitful in so far as it arises from that relationship and is led by His Spirit. Having a close relationship with God enables us to receive revelation and understanding from Him so that we respond to others as He wants us to. As we live close to Him, we will touch others with His love and understanding and demonstrate forgiveness and mercy. Through living close to Him, our prayers for others will be led by His Spirit and will focus on the power of God to restore.

Throughout the epistles, we are continually encouraged by the Spirit to believe that we are children of God,

---

37 Acts 2, 4:31; 2 Corinthians 12:9; Ephesians 3:16, 6: 10; Philippians 4:13.
38 Luke 4:14.
39 John 1:33-34; Matthew 3:11,16-17.
40 For further passages giving insight on baptism in the Holy Spirit you may like to read Acts 2, 8, 9, 10, 19.

"The Spirit you received does not make you slaves, so that you live in fear again; rather, the Spirit you received brought about your adoption to sonship. And by him we cry, 'Abba, Father.' The Spirit himself testifies with our spirit that we are God's children." Romans 8:15-16

Being a child of God is the most awesome relationship we can have. When Jesus calls us to follow Him, He is inviting us to join the mysterious and marvellous relationship at the heart of the Godhead.

Chapter 1:5

Our New Identity in Christ

"Therefore, if any man be in Christ, he is a new creature: old things are passed away; behold, all things are become new." 2 Corinthians 5:17

Since God made us in His image, we are spirit and have a soul. In this world, we have a physical body within which the spirit and soul live, but the physical body is not who we are, even though it is uniquely ours. The soul is not who we are, although it reveals our personality and character. When Jesus comes into our lives, our spirits are renewed through the indwelling Holy Spirit. We have a new nature that is able to resist sin, and through which God guides and teaches us. We also have a will with the desire to obey and follow Jesus, a mind which is the mind of Christ, and we bear the fruit of the Spirit.[41] As soon as we are born again in our spirits, we have this new identity in Christ with its accompanying blessings and benefits,

> *"See what great love the Father has lavished on us, that we should be called children of God! And that is what we are!"* 1 John 3:1

Thus, it is our spirits that reveal who we are. Once we grasp that because our true identity is in Christ, that our righteousness in Christ is a gift and not earned by our own efforts, and that our souls are undergoing a work of transformation, we can reconcile the apparent contradiction

---

41 Galatians 5:22-23.

between what we know about our sinfulness and what God says about us in Scripture. Living from our new identity enables us to believe that we can do all that God has planned for us to do, because it is based upon the security of being a child of God, and on knowing that we are equipped by God,

> *"For we are God's handiwork, created in Christ Jesus to do good works, which God prepared in advance for us to do."* Ephesians 2:10

We become channels through which His Spirit can minister to us and through us.

Once we receive the Spirit of God and of Jesus, we receive His *"zōé"* life; the full, abundant, never-ending life that Jesus talks about in John 10:10. This is truth. Any insecurity and any inferiority that we feel about ourselves comes from our souls and our former way of thinking and behaving before we were born anew. God says we are a new creation, and that is what we are. God says we have a new nature, and we do - His divine nature. The question arises in many minds as to why so many of us still struggle with poor self-image and insecurity even after we invite Jesus into our lives. Perhaps, instead of believing the truth that we are a new creation, we are continuing to think as we always have. What would help us to change from our old patterns of thought and behaviour?

Our souls also have a mind, emotions and will which have previously operated independently of God and which follow our own reasonings, desires and choices. They now need to be brought into alignment with our spirits which are guided by Jesus. What this means is that not only have our souls to learn new truths and a new way of thinking, but they need to be restored from the effects of previous harmful experiences and our responses to these, and from inherited generational family beliefs, attitudes and behaviours. We are to demolish these old ways of thinking[42]

---

42 2 Corinthians 10:3-5.

and be transformed in the way we think,[43] but we find that we are not able to do this in our own strength. Only as we meditate on the Word of God, looking to Jesus to help us and following the Spirit's promptings, will we be given the grace to accomplish this. It is a new way of living, with Jesus as our focus and at the centre of our lives.

Our enemy, satan, accuses us non-stop, and we all hear the inner voice of condemnation, feeling that a great deal of the time we don't measure up. If we don't know how to deal with this, we will struggle throughout our lives. The truth is that in Christ, we are righteous because of what Christ did, and so it's not a case of one moment we're in, the next we're out, then we're in again, according to our behaviour. There is no condemnation for those who are in Christ Jesus,[44] and so we're in right standing with God all the time, even though we mess up. We are perfected forever in Christ. Every day we must believe that our sins were taken and that our identity comes from Jesus who is sin-free. Righteousness is a gift, and just as we cannot receive it through our own efforts, neither can we lose it through our sinful behaviour. This does not mean that because of this we can do as we please and expect there will not be any consequences because we still have a law of sowing and reaping which takes effect in our lives here on earth.[45] God loves each one of us and likes to bless us. It is wise to keep reminding ourselves of this and recall that all His thoughts towards us are good.

---

43 Romans 12:1-2.
44 Romans 8:1.
45 Galatians 6:7.

Chapter 1:6

Gifts from Father, Son and Holy Spirit

"There are diversities of gifts, but the same Spirit. And there are diversities of activities, but it is the same God who works all in all. There are differences of ministries, but the same Lord." 1 Corinthians 12:4-6

How does God equip us through His Holy Spirit so that we can be fruitful in building up the body of Christ and in being effective witnesses? What does it mean to be part of the body of Christ?

When we receive Jesus as Saviour and Lord, He comes to live within us by His Spirit, and our bodies become a temple of the Holy Spirit. We are brought into the family of God, become part of the body of Christ, and enter into a relationship with Jesus as the bride of Christ. All these metaphors help us understand different aspects of the consequences of our new birth.

Under the Old Covenant, the Holy Spirit was given to specific people for a specific reason and for a specified time, e.g., to prophets such as Elijah[46] and Elisha,[47] to priests such as Aaron and to kings such as Saul[48] and David.[49] There is, however, an interesting reference in Numbers 11:26-29, where we are told that two elders, Eldad and Medad, prophesied

---

46 2 Kings 2:9.
47 2 Kings2:15.
48 1 Samuel 10.
49 1 Samuel 16:1-13.

because the Spirit rested on them. Moses exclaimed that he wished God would put His Spirit on all people that they might prophesy.

As time passed, the Prophets told of a time when God would send His Spirit upon all men and women. He made it clear that this Spirit within their hearts/spirits would direct them in God's ways and be a sign to them that they were His people.[50] Joel prophesied[51] of a time when God's Spirit would be poured out on all people, and sons and daughters would prophesy, old men have dreams, and young men have visions.

Jesus described the Spirit as the Spirit of Jesus and of the Father, as the Counsellor, and as the One who would empower for witness.[52] Since our bodies are the temple of the Holy Spirit,[53] we can expect the Spirit to impart gifts of grace through us to build up the body of Christ and so witness to the unbeliever. We can expect the Holy Spirit to work through us in His power, bringing healing and performing miracles.

It is within the context of belonging to the body of Christ that God equips His people for service and witness. We do not live the Christian life solo, but because we have been brought up in a society that encourages the individual to climb the ladder, to succeed for personal acclamation, and to focus on bettering their circumstances, we may find that we need to work on changing ingrained mindsets. A mindset based on "me" and "my service for God" needs to be exchanged for a mindset based on the understanding that God's people work together as a team, with no-one more important than another, no-one less important. When we focus on the "me", all sorts of issues arise, such as insecurities, potential for pride, and jealousy. When we understand the concept of being part of the body of Christ, working together to build up the Church, we are set free from our personal misgivings and become empowered in Christ, encouraged as part of a vibrant, Spirit-filled Church worldwide.

---

50 Ezekiel 36:25-28.
51 Joel 2:28-32.
52 John 16.
53 1 Corinthians 6:19.

In Scripture, many gifts are mentioned, all of which come from God.[54]

There are gifts given by Jesus to the Church and for the building up of the Church,

> *"So Christ himself gave the apostles, the prophets, the evangelists, the pastors and teachers, to equip his people for works of service, so that the body of Christ may be built up until we all reach unity in the faith and in the knowledge of the Son of God and become mature, attaining to the whole measure of the fullness of Christ."* Ephesians 4:11-13

They demonstrate the love of Jesus for His Church, and His desire that she enter into fullness in Christ and reach out to others in service.

God the Father has created each one of us with gifts with which we can serve Him and one another; gifts such as mercy, administration, serving, teaching, leadership and hospitality. And we are instructed,

> *"Each of you should use whatever gift you have received to serve others, as faithful stewards of God's grace in its various forms."* 1 Peter 4:10

The Father's gifts to us equip us for the plans He has for our lives and give us purpose.

There are nine miraculous gifts given by the Holy Spirit listed in 1 Corinthians 12:8-11. They reveal that everything the Holy Spirit does and wants to do through us is good, kind, gracious and loving. These nine differ from those given by Jesus and by God the Father in that they are not resident within us but are given by the Holy Spirit to every believer as their relationship with Jesus Christ begins and develops. They are distributed to individuals within the body as and when He wills, and for the good of the whole.[55] Each gift of the Spirit is for the purpose of

---

54 James 1:17.
55 1 Corinthians 12:8-10.

glorifying God by pointing to the essential reality and nature of Jesus and for the purpose of building up the Church which is the body of Christ. This picture of the body of Christ in whom the Spirit of Jesus dwells, reveals how God draws us into unity in the body as a diversity of many parts.[56] It shows us the love and forgiveness of God in Christ Jesus and enables us to respond in repentance and love towards Him and towards one another. Paul reminds us of the importance of love[57] and encourages us to,

"Follow the way of love and eagerly desire the spiritual gifts."
1 Corinthians 14:1

The body of Christ is the context in which the Holy Spirit gives us His gifts. They are gifts and not trophies.

"All these are the work of one and the same Spirit, and He distributes them to each one, just as he determines." 1 Corinthians 12:11

Gifts alone are not a sign of spiritual maturity. Spiritually mature people are recognised by their fruit,

"The fruit of the Spirit is love, joy, peace, patience, kindness, goodness, faithfulness, gentleness and self-control." Galatians 5:22-23

As we live in relationship with God and He cultivates a Christ-like character in us we increasingly display the fruit of the Holy Spirit.

These Spirit-gifts are not for personal gratification but for the good of the body and for witness, as 1 Corinthians 12:7,

"Now to each one the manifestation of the Spirit is given for the common good."

---

56 1 Corinthians 12:12-27.
57 1 Corinthians 13.

Every believer can expect to be given one or more of these gifts from time to time to minister in particular situations as needed. As we mature as Christians, we can expect to grow in the measure of faith we have to use these gifts, and, over time, we will increasingly function in a naturally supernatural way. Note that scripture makes it clear that it is possible to have powerful gifts and to lack love and grace. Gifts without love are worthless,

"I may be able to speak with the languages of men and angels...I may have the gift of prophecy...I may have knowledge...and faith to move mountains...but if I have not love, I am nothing...it does no good." 1 Corinthians 13:1-3

What are the Gifts of the Holy Spirit?
Paul writes,

"To one there is given through the Spirit the message of wisdom, to another the message of knowledge by means of the same Spirit, to another faith by the same Spirit, to another gifts of healing by that one Spirit, to another miraculous powers, to another prophecy, to another distinguishing between spirits, to another speaking in different kinds of tongues, and to still another the interpretation of tongues. All these are the work of one and the same Spirit, and He gives them to each one, just as He determines." 1 Corinthians 12:8-10

The Message of Wisdom
The miraculous gift of wisdom is noted by its spontaneity. It suddenly appears - after all, it's a gift - and has an ability to end confusion or disagreement by cutting through and giving a solution. It does not arise from man's experience but from God's Spirit. Examples in Scripture are Solomon giving a wise ruling,[58] Jesus' answer about paying taxes to Caesar[59] and Jesus' use of parables to give His listeners understanding.

---

58 1 Kings 3:16-28.
59 Matthew 22:15-22.

When we are in a tricky situation where we don't know what to say or do, we may be given the gift of wisdom. James, in his letter, encourages us to ask God for wisdom.[60] A Christian friend of mine was at a dinner party where those seated near her were discussing different religions. As she listened to the conversation, words rose up from her spirit, words which were truth and against which no-one could argue. *"Christianity is a relationship, not a religion,"* she said. One time when I was pondering the use of structures in a church setting and whether they allowed the Holy Spirit to have freedom, I sensed these words rising from my spirit, *"It's not the structures that are an offence to God but the pride in these."* Often, wisdom is given to guide us in the use of the other gifts. For example, I have often asked God for the gift of wisdom in response to receiving a word of knowledge given within a ministry context. This is so that I avoid the possibility of bringing condemnation on anyone, e.g., rather than confront someone with whether they have unforgiveness, I ask them whether they are struggling with hurt caused by someone.

The Message of Knowledge

The gift of a 'word,' or words of knowledge, enables us to know something we do not already know. It may be described as 'the mind of Christ' being manifested to the mind of the believer and is given when needed in a moment of time,

> *"Who has known the mind of the Lord so as to instruct him? But we have the mind of Christ."* 1 Corinthians 2:16

It may be a revelation of facts, present, past or future, which have not been known previously by the natural mind of the person. This gift is given to protect God's people, to help us to pray more effectively, and to enable us to help others. We see this gift in operation when Jesus met with the Samaritan woman at the well[61] and when He called upon Zacchaeus.[62]

---

60 James 1:5.
61 John 4:16-19.
62 Luke 19:5.

There are many ways in which to receive a word of knowledge, and it's not always through words. It may be given through pictures, impressions, dreams, visions, trances, Scripture, tongues and interpretation, smell, or touch. A word of knowledge is not limited to spiritual or church concerns but can be given anywhere within any situation, e.g., in car mechanics, in painting or writing, or in domestic affairs. When the Israelites were building the Temple, God said of Bezalel,

"I have filled him with the Spirit of God, with wisdom, with understanding, with knowledge and with all kinds of skills - to make artistic designs for work in gold, silver and bronze, to cut and set stones, to work in wood, and to engage in all kinds of crafts."
Exodus 31:3-5

God has spoken to me many times through dreams. Sometimes it is to give me insight and understanding within the context of ministry, as when I dreamt of a client being held upside down by his Achilles heel. When I awoke and asked God what the dream was about, He told me that this man appeared to be strong, but he had a weakness – his insecurity. This was his "Achilles heel". In another dream, I was subject to attack by gunfighters shooting. Each time I darted to a different hiding place, a round of bullets was fired towards my previous position. I marvelled at the fact that I escaped each time just as bullets were being fired. One of the times, I was splattered with some purplish-blue liquid, and when I looked back to where I had been, I saw a tall flat thing like a radiator had been struck, and this same liquid was smeared over the radiator in the form of a cross. Then I saw the colour red being added and knew that it represented the blood of Christ. I became aware as I was awakening that I was rehearsing in my mind the importance of the Cross and the Blood as my protection so that I wouldn't forget.

Within the context of ministry and when praying for people, I ask God for words of knowledge so that I can understand how to proceed in ministry or how to pray for people and situations. I have listed some of the ways through which God speaks to me on pages 196-197 in this book. As you read through all the books in the series, *The Ministry of the Father's Heart*, you will find many examples.

The Gift of Faith

The gift of faith is given in a situation to enable the person to move with God in what He wants to do. It brings conviction that God is about to act. Like all the gifts of the Spirit, it is given, received, used, and accomplishes that for which it is given. This gift enables us to connect with heaven and become a conduit of power from God to man. It overrules doubts and hindrances we may have in our hearts and minds, enabling us to move with the faith of God. There are many examples in Scripture. The Centurion[63] and the woman with the haemorrhage[64] are both commended for their faith. Faith in God is necessary if healing is to take place. Where God wants to perform a miracle, He will often release the gift of faith, or give words of knowledge leading to faith that indicate that healing or something extraordinary is about to take place. In many churches, members of the Prayer Ministry Teams spend time before the services, praying and listening to God for His insights. Where these are received in the congregation, faith does its work, expectancy is raised, and healing follows. An example of this in our fellowship was where a mother was given the gift of faith when she heard a word of knowledge about a club foot and went for prayer for her baby.

When God was calling me into full-time ministry, He used several approaches to build up my faith concerning the coming change. Two years before I embarked on this ministry, someone who didn't know me told me he believed that God had told him I would be a "counsellor of patience." At the time, I didn't know what this meant, and it was only after many years in ministry that I understood. About this time also, on several occasions God highlighted Isaiah 61:1 when I was reading, and on two occasions gave this verse to different people to pass on to me as a message from Him. He spoke to me through my daily readings

63 Luke 7:2-9.
64 Luke 8:43-48.

and prompted three people to ask me whether I had ever considered going into full-time pastoral ministry in the church. Every step of the way I tested whether it was God who was directing me, and I received many confirmations.

Gifts of Healing
There are many gifts of healing. Sometimes a person may find that they are frequently used by God as a conduit in healing specific ailments. Sometimes, this gift may be more general, leading to many different ailments being healed through any one person. Scripture records many healings. Present-day examples within our fellowship, but not exclusive to it, are the healing of painful backs, healing from arthritis (rheumatoid arthritis and osteoarthritis), healing of sprained ankles, painful knees, healing from cancer.

Miraculous Powers
A miracle is an event which is inexplicable by the laws of nature and so held to be an act of God. Miracles are often not recognised as such. Thirty-seven miracles performed by Jesus that are recorded in the Gospels drew people to Him, revealing His divine nature and causing many to glorify God. Examples today are people coming to faith in Jesus, instant healings, pregnancies that defy medical prognosis, raising from the dead, stilling storms, multiplication of resources, and deliverances. There are many examples of miracles occurring all over the world. One time when I was travelling from work through Belfast, I rounded a corner only to find that the road layout had been changed. As I braked to a halt before red traffic lights, I squeezed into the only space, one between two cars in two adjacent lanes. I still marvel at the way in which God provided for me and my car that day, and I'm quite sure that He has protected me many times when I have not been aware of the danger.

The Gift of Prophecy
Prophecy is most often in the form of encouragement from God to a person or group. Sometimes it gives insight, guiding us in understanding

the ways of God, and sometimes it gives guidance for intercession. At other times it is given to confirm the path that a person is taking. We offer anything we believe God is telling us with an open hand, inviting the person or group to test the words for themselves. No-one should ever make a decision based on another's word of prophecy, as God will always guide the person directly. We need to take into account that God's timing is not always the same as we think it should be and we ought to seek Him further about it. In prayer meetings, where we spend time worshipping God and allowing Him to set the agenda, we have sometimes been given words of prophecy which have come to pass at a later date, some of which we may not have recognised as prophetic at the time. An example of this was when I was given a picture of a high-rise block of flats on fire and people hanging out the windows screaming for help. Two years later, God reminded me of this revelation when Grenfell Tower flats in London went on fire.

In October 2020, during a time when we were enjoying a degree of freedom after the lockdown because of Covid 19, I received these words through the Spirit, "*Nestle in. The storm's coming. You are under the safety of My wings, My child. Do not fear though the enemy attack, for it cannot come near you. Don't take thought for the morrow, what you shall wear or what you shall eat or drink. Live today to the full, enjoying My love and My presence.*" Then the words of a song[65] were followed by these words, "*A storm is brewing, the like of which has never been seen before. It is a storm of hatred and violence whipped up by the enemy of your souls. Have nothing to do with it. Live humbly in My presence. People will mock, they will trample over your vineyards, but I will be with you.*" For me, the significance of the word "vineyards" lies in it being a reference to our inner life, our heart. In Song of Songs, the Shulamite had neglected her vineyard and was full of fear. As the story unfolds, she seeks the Shepherd's presence, and through spending time with Him she tends her "vineyard" and moves out from fear and into love. I believe that God was telling me that the coming storm had the potential to fill people

---

65 Hide me now, Still, Reuben Morgan, Hillsong Worship

with fear, but if they prepared themselves by spending time drawing close to God and getting to know Him better, they would not live in fear but be filled with His love and peace. Since then, we have seen increasing violence and hatred released throughout the world. Only when we are secure in the love of God can we battle from a place of safety in Jesus against what the enemy throws at us, and only when we battle according to God's leading will we break through the enemy's plans. God entrusts us to use His insights when we pray.

Distinguishing Between Spirits
The gift of discerning of spirits is important as there are many deceiving spirits around us, and this gift enables us to recognise whether something is of God or not. It is useful when, as part of the body of Christ, we are listening to teaching of the Word. In the world, too, it is important for us to be able to discern whether what we are being told is deception or truth.

This gift also reveals which evil spirit may be harassing a person, thereby helping us to free those who are being influenced by a demonic spirit and giving us insight into the realm of satan. Paul discerned the spirit of divination in the slave girl[66] and was annoyed by it but chose to wait a few days before addressing it. This shows us that we don't always have to act immediately on what we encounter, but we should seek God's timing. It's not that we are to tolerate sin, etc., but we are not to "play God" either. When we discern something evil, we should seek God and find out whether He wants us to take any action or remain in prayer. Frequently I have been shown which spirit is driving a person into behaviour that they want to stop. An example of this was a person who wanted to stop gambling. I was able to discern when he was telling me the truth and when he was attempting to deceive me, an extremely useful gift in this context.

In ministry, this gift, along with the gift of knowledge, has proved necessary and invaluable and has led to many people being healed from

66 Acts 16:17.

various traumas. Discernment can also be given to help us to know a person as Jesus does.

"So, from now on we regard no one from a worldly point of view.
Though we once regarded Christ in this way, we do so no longer."
2 Corinthians 5:16

Knowing a person from God's perspective frees us to bless and pray for a person, even when hurt by them. In wider world terms, this gift also gives us insight as to how God perceives our country and others, thus leading us in how to pray.

The Gift of Different Kinds of Tongues

All the gifts of the Spirit are released through us only with our collaboration and require us to step out in trust in God. This gift is different from the others in that the words imparted to us are not in our native lingo but are words from a foreign language,[67] or the tongues of angels.[68] It is the only gift of the Holy Spirit that can be used to build up the individual as well as to build up the body of Christ and to witness.

As the tongue is an unruly member in our bodies[69] and can be used in so many hurtful ways, it is significant that God has chosen the gift of tongues as one of the ways in which He brings conviction of sin, helps us to change, enables us to be built up at a personal level, and heals our hearts. Through this gift, He can lead us into worshipping Jesus, and if we ask for the interpretation, we sometimes know directly that He is encouraging us (The gift of interpreting tongues is explained later). Praying in the Spirit keeps us in God's love.[70]

On occasion, when I have spoken in tongues during ministry, this has calmed someone who was frightened and helped them receive

---

67 Acts 2: 1-11
68 1 Corinthians 13:1
69 James 3:1-12.
70 Jude 1:20-21.

peace. At other times when praying in tongues over a person, they were healed physically. I have also found that when used in deliverance, I am aware that the tongue has changed and seems to carry authority. Jackie Pullinger, a missionary to Hong Kong, in her work among drug addicts, found that praying in tongues led to remarkable deliverances and to them coming off drugs without withdrawal symptoms.

Praying in the Spirit frequently triggers off other gifts. For example, after praying in tongues I often find that I am given a word of knowledge or a word of wisdom or that my faith has heightened.

A friend told me of an occasion when she went to speak to a man who was waiting in a hospital outpatients department and looking worried. It quickly became evident that he couldn't understand her, so she quietly prayed in the Spirit, and to her surprise, the gentleman in question understood what she was saying. This demonstrates the use of tongues as a sign and an encouragement to the unbeliever.

It is a wonderful gift with endless possibilities for good as it gives complete freedom to the Holy Spirit to pray through us according to the will of God and so to determine an outcome.[71] Above all, it releases us into deep worship at times when we find it difficult to express our adoration vocally to God. At such times, within a gathering of God's people, it can be almost ethereal as we join in the cadences and harmonies of the Spirit, sometimes praise swelling up and soaring, and at other times, fading into quietness, only to be stirred up again by the One who leads us to worship Jesus.

The Gift of Interpretation of Tongues

When we are praising God in tongues, there is no need for interpretation as we are addressing God, but when the Holy Spirit uses the gift of tongues in public to speak into the hearts of His children, we must ask Him for the interpretation. Sometimes this gift of interpretation is

---

71 Romans 8:26-27.

released through the person who has spoken in the unknown tongue, sometimes it's through another. The message may be for the whole body or an individual. It is exciting to witness those in the body of Christ building one another up in such a way. I have often spoken in tongues over someone and then experienced God releasing the interpretation through me. Sometimes, in a meeting where we are praying, I may be quietly praying in tongues and then find that I am led to speak out the interpretation or words of prophecy.

As a final word on the use of these gifts of the Spirit, I want to point to the chapter at the heart of Paul's instructions to the Corinthian Church about the gifts of the Spirit. Sandwiched between the two main chapters on the gifts, 1 Corinthians 12 and 14, is this wonderful, well-loved Scripture,

"If I speak in the tongues of men or of angels, but do not have love, I am only a resounding gong or a clanging cymbal. If I have the gift of prophecy and can fathom all mysteries and all knowledge, and if I have a faith that can move mountains, but do not have love, I am nothing. If I give all I possess to the poor and give over my body to hardship that I may boast, but do not have love, I gain nothing. Love is patient, love is kind. It does not envy, it does not boast, it is not proud. It does not dishonour others, it is not self-seeking, it is not easily angered, it keeps no record of wrongs. Love does not delight in evil but rejoices with the truth. It always protects, always trusts, always hopes, always perseveres. Love never fails. But where there are prophecies, they will cease; where there are tongues, they will be stilled; where there is knowledge, it will pass away. For we know in part and we prophesy in part, but when completeness comes, what is in part disappears. When I was a child, I talked like a child, I thought like a child, I reasoned like a child. When I became a man, I put the ways of childhood behind me. For now, we see only a reflection as in a mirror; then we shall see face to face. Now I know in part;

then I shall know fully, even as I am fully known. And now these three remain: faith, hope and love. But the greatest of these is love."
1 Corinthians 13:1-13

Growing in Faith in God

"But you, dear friends, by building yourselves up in your most holy faith and praying in the Holy Spirit, keep yourselves in God's love as you wait for the mercy of our Lord Jesus Christ to bring you to eternal life."
Jude 20, 21

The faith that we have in Christ Jesus and in His promises to us as His disciples is a gift of grace from God,

> *"For by grace you have been saved through faith, and that not of yourselves; it is the gift of God, not of works, lest anyone should boast."*
> Ephesians 2:8

It is the Holy Spirit who draws us into this faith, giving each of us *"a measure of faith…"*

> *"For I say, through the grace given to me, to everyone who is among you, not to think of himself more highly than he ought to think, but to think soberly, as God has dealt to each a measure of faith."*
> Romans 12:3

This measure of faith releases the life of heaven within us and begins a work of grace. What we believe in our spirits streams into our hearts, has a profound effect on our lives, and flows out into the world. Jesus had this to say,

"A good man brings good things out of the good stored up in his heart, and an evil man brings evil things out of the evil stored up in his heart. For the mouth speaks what the heart is full of." Luke 6:45

We are exhorted to,

"Above all else, guard your heart, for everything you do flows from it." Proverbs 4:23

This implies that our hearts are like the control centres for our lives.

Information is stored in our minds and, if meditated upon, becomes a heart belief. Because we want to have beliefs that enable us to trust God without wavering, it is important that we feed our minds with the truths of Scripture; then, as we meditate on them, they become settled in our hearts as beliefs. These deeply held heart beliefs control to what extent we live by faith. If, when we ask God for something, we then waver between trust and doubt, we will not receive. James writes,

"But when you ask, you must believe and not doubt, because the one who doubts is like a wave of the sea, blown and tossed by the wind. That person should not expect to receive anything from the Lord. Such a person is double-minded and unstable in all they do." James 1:6-8

God wants to help us change from being double-minded with a divided heart into people of faith who trust God completely. This is why Paul urges us,

"Let the message of Christ dwell among you richly as you teach and admonish one another with all wisdom through psalms, hymns, and songs from the Spirit, singing to God with gratitude in your hearts. And whatever you do, whether in word or deed, do it all in the name of the Lord Jesus, giving thanks to God the Father through him." Colossians 3:16-17

"So then, just as you received Christ Jesus as Lord, continue to live your lives in him, rooted and built up in him, strengthened in the faith as you were taught, and overflowing with thankfulness." Colossians 2:6-7

As we read, reflect and meditate upon the Word of God, these truths become rooted within our hearts, producing a bountiful crop even though we do not see it grow,

"The Kingdom of God is like a farmer who scatters seed on the ground. Night and day, while he's asleep or awake, the seed sprouts and grows, but he does not understand how it happens. The earth produces the crops on its own. First a leaf blade pushes through, then the heads of wheat are formed, and finally the grain ripens." Mark 4:26-28

While we sleep, our minds subconsciously continue to process and feed into our hearts what they have been exposed to throughout the day. In this parable, the heart is likened to the earth in that it doesn't recognise the type of seed sown but just grows it. This means that whatever we feed our minds with during the day, whether good or bad, may be taking root in our hearts and steadily growing. So one of the ways in which we can guard our hearts is through being careful about what we are feeding them through the three gateways into the heart; our eyes, ears and mouths.

Our faith in God does not grow through merely reading the Bible as a source of information or as history or biography, nor does it grow through merely learning verses. These all contribute to growing our faith but are not enough of themselves. Some people may know the Bible, chapter and verse, but may not know the God of the Bible. Our faith in God grows through meeting Jesus and seeing Him revealed in the words as we meditate on them; what we call "rhema" words or "Spirit-breathed words." As we read slowly, the revelation from God is like a light going on in our souls,

"Faith comes by hearing and hearing by the word of God."
Romans 10:1

Such revelation leads to personal knowledge and understanding of God and His ways which, in turn, increases our faith in Him.

As we approach each book of the Bible, asking why this book was written, what its purpose was, and to whom was it written, we can discover the heart of Jesus and how He reaches out to meet the needs of people. For example, we might ask ourselves why the first letter to the Thessalonians was written and conclude that, under the inspiration of the Holy Spirit, Paul was addressing a fear that the people had because they were going through a terrible time of persecution. Far away from them, Paul was concerned about these Christians because he had heard that they believed that the tribulation had come and that Jesus had come and gone. Paul wrote to assure them that he was still there and that, by implication, Jesus had not come for His people. In the second letter, he goes on to explain what will happen when Jesus does return and strengthens them with advice. In all of this, we see the heart of Jesus wanting to comfort and instruct His people. Every story is a revelation about Jesus, His love, mercy, grace, justice, forgiveness, wisdom and wrath at evil.

Our own faith grows each time we hear His rhema Word to us personally. When God speaks to us, whether it is through the Bible or through words of knowledge or visions, dreams etc., and we know that we know that it is He who has spoken, then nothing can shake our confidence in the truth of what we have heard. No matter what we face, no matter the timing, when we know that Jesus has spoken, we believe. Faith, based on such revelation, is rock solid. It's as though revelation from the Spirit lights up the path ahead, and so faith remains strong. The story of Abraham's life inspires us to trust God as he did. He heard God speak, believed Him and obeyed,

"The Lord had said to Abraham, 'Leave your country, your people and your father's household and go to the land I show you. I will make you into a great nation and I will bless you; I will make your name great, and you will be a blessing. I will bless those who bless you, and whoever curses you I will curse; and all the peoples of the earth will be blessed through you." Genesis 12:1-3

It's worth taking the time to reflect on the enormity of this move. Abraham wasn't told where he was going,

"By faith, Abraham, when called to go to a place he would later receive as his inheritance, obeyed and went, even though he did not know where he was going." Hebrews 11:8

He received a revelation from God, but did not know or understand the where or why or how. He simply obeyed, which is, itself, an act of faith. The key here was that he had received revelation from the One with whom he had a relationship. Paul writes that it is *"faith working through love"* that avails.[72] The outcome of faith applied is the fruit of faith and, as fruit, it reproduces itself in more faith, both in the person exercising it and in those observing it at work.

God frequently warns his people about serving God and mammon, the consequence of a divided heart. As long as we live in this way or struggle with two opposing beliefs about something, we will not be able to move forward with faith and so will not receive the fruit of faith. We are encouraged to have,

"an inherent trust and enduring confidence in the power, wisdom and goodness of God." Hebrews 11:3 AMP

We will then witness miracles, healings and a multitude of blessings and receive inner strength to face the difficult times. Faith grows as we find Jesus to be faithful to us in our everyday lives. When we are in distress, we find that He is steady; He is the Rock.

---

72 Galatians 5:6.

"To learn strong faith is to endure great trials. I have learned my faith by standing firm amid severe testing."[ix]

Paul taught that when there are hardships in life, the purpose is not to try to avoid them but to face them head-on with the strength that comes from Christ,

> *"I will boast all the more gladly of my weaknesses, so that the power of Christ may rest upon me."* 2 Corinthians 12:9

James assured us that,

> *"The testing of your faith [through experience] produces endurance [leading to spiritual maturity, and inner peace] ."* James 1:3 AMP

What is our part?

> *"We must keep our eyes on Jesus, who leads us and makes our faith complete. He endured the shame of being nailed to a cross, because he knew later on he would be glad he did. Now he is seated at the right side of God's throne!"* Hebrews 12:2 CEV

> *"Blessed is the man who trusts in the Lord and whose hope is in the Lord. For he shall be like a tree planted by the waters, which spreads out its root by the river, and will not fear when heat comes: but its leaf will be green, and will not be anxious in the year of drought, nor will cease from yielding fruit."* Jeremiah 17:7-8 NKJV

> *"Trust in and rely confidently on the Lord with all your heart and do not rely on your own insight or understanding. In all your ways know and acknowledge and recognise him, and he will make your paths straight and smooth [removing obstacles that block your way]."* Proverbs 3:5-6 AMP

True heart faith in God is not

o   a whipping up of our emotions
o   mind control
o   presumption
o   guided by circumstances or by the news
o   based on people's opinions

It is the faith in God that has been reawakened in our spirits when they were regenerated, and which grows in our hearts as we transform our minds through the Word of God.

Even when faith is steadily growing, that faith can be short-circuited by unbelief in some area. Jesus has this to say,

> *"Whoever says to this mountain, 'Be removed and be cast into the sea', and does not doubt in his heart, but believes that those things he says will be done, he will have whatever he says."* Mark 11:23

Our faith must be stubborn in the face of opposition. Jesus told those gathered at the foot of the Mount of Transfiguration that the reason the boy was not healed was because of their unbelief. He told them that they needed faith like a grain of mustard seed, the kind of faith that perseveres no matter what faces us.[73]

An Example of Heroic Faith
Jim Elliot and his wife, Elisabeth, are examples of those who lived by faith. Jim, a missionary in Ecuador, was killed by the natives. We may wonder how we can reconcile this brutal murder with God's promise that,

> *"No weapon forged against you will prevail, and you will refute every tongue that accuses you. This is the heritage of the servants of the Lord, and this is their vindication from me, declares the Lord."* Isaiah 54:17

---

73 Matthew 17:20.

With our human understanding, we see Jim killed by weapons forged against him. So, did God not keep the promise within this verse? Faith believes that God is always good and, whatever the facts, a good God allowed this. There comes a time for each of us when the body dies, but what is important is what happens to the "me" bit of me. Jim is now with God for all eternity. No weapon forged against him prevailed as nothing was able to destroy his relationship with Jesus and His destiny.

We are confident that God walked with Jim through his suffering and with his family through their suffering, perhaps teaching them more about His love for them but also about His love for those who had murdered Jim. Here was a man, prepared beforehand by God to answer this call and share the Gospel amongst a people who did not know Him, but also here was a child of God deeply loved by God going to certain death. Jim only saw the potential for others to come to know Jesus and did not count the cost to himself. It is wise for us to reflect on the pain that God probably felt as He called Jim Elliot to the mission field, knowing that suffering lay ahead.

If we are to continue trusting God in all circumstances, we need to base our understanding not on our perceptions but on who God is, that He is good and that He chooses what is best. Then, even when we find it difficult to understand, we can still trust Him. In those times, we demonstrate faith in God and in His ways.

Jim's wife, Elisabeth, chose to trust God despite all that had happened. She continued to demonstrate a steady faith in God no matter what He asked her to do, believing that He saw beyond what her natural eye could see. Elisabeth was drawn so close to Jesus that she saw the murderers as Jesus saw them, as people that He loved and died for, and she felt drawn to go and show them the love and forgiveness of Jesus. She was in a unique place to be able to do this and was received by the very people-group that had killed her husband. Eventually, she had the joy of baptising the man who had killed him.

There are many examples of faith quoted in Hebrews 11. It is worthwhile pondering the faith that these people had, a faith that frequently didn't receive the promised outcome in this life. Faith doesn't have to get but believes without seeing the promised outcome physically. Faith is content in the waiting because faith is in God and what He has said and not in what is seen.

Our faith can be such a natural thing for us that we move in it without really thinking about it simply because we have an ongoing relationship with Jesus. Day by day, we talk to Him about everything, pray for ourselves and others, and believe and rely on Him to protect, provide for and guide us. These are each an outworking of our faith. Through our calm faith and through our presence and love, we can strengthen and inspire one another in faith.

When Abraham asked God questions, it was in an effort to understand and not because he didn't have faith. When we ask God questions to understand what He is saying, He answers and, in so doing, helps us towards obeying. In fact, revelation is often a precursor to our being able to exercise faith in a specific situation. When we move in obedience to God and trust in Him, He confirms His trustworthiness and gives us confirmations from time to time to encourage our ongoing faith in Him.

Points for Reflection

o   Think of times when you showed faith by words or actions
    or in the way you live.
o   Recall some examples of when someone exercised faith on
    your behalf.
o   Recall some examples of when you exercised faith on
    behalf of someone else.
o   Does any Scripture promise cause some kind of resistance
    to rise up within you? This may indicate a heart belief that
    needs to be changed.

Scriptures give us further insights on strengthening our faith,

"But you, beloved, build yourselves up on [the foundation of] your most holy faith [continually progress, rise like an edifice higher and higher], pray in the Holy Spirit, and keep yourselves in the love of God, waiting anxiously and looking forward to the mercy of our Lord Jesus Christ [which will bring you] to eternal life. And have mercy on some, who are doubting; save others, snatching them out of the fire; and on some have mercy but with fear, loathing even the clothing spotted and polluted by their shameless immoral freedom. Now to Him who is able to keep you from stumbling or falling into sin, and to present you unblemished [blameless and faultless] in the presence of His glory with triumphant joy and unspeakable delight, to the only God our Saviour, through Jesus Christ our Lord, be glory, majesty, dominion, and power, before all time and now and forever Amen." Jude 20 AMP

"Then, because you belong to Christ Jesus, God will bless you with peace that no one can completely understand. And this peace will control the way you think and feel. Finally, my friends, keep your minds on whatever is true, pure, right, holy, friendly, and proper. Don't ever stop thinking about what is truly worthwhile and worthy of praise." Philippians 4:7-8 CEV

We are to strengthen ourselves and one another by praying in the Holy Spirit,

"In the same way, the Spirit helps us in our weakness. We do not know what we ought to pray for, but the Spirit himself intercedes for us through wordless groans. And he who searches our hearts knows the mind of the Spirit, because the Spirit intercedes for God's people in accordance with the will of God." Romans 8:26-27

We are to keep ourselves in the love of God,

*"For you have not received a spirit of slavery leading again to fear
[of God's judgment], but you have received the Spirit of adoption
as sons [the Spirit producing sonship] by which we [joyfully] cry;
"Abba! Father!" The Spirit Himself testifies and confirms together
with our spirit [assuring us] that we [believers] are children of God."*
Romans 8:15-16 AMP

*"I am the vine, you are the branches; he who abides in Me and I in
Him, he bears much fruit, for apart from Me you can do nothing."*
John 15:5

We are to pray and praise God in all circumstances,

*"Rejoice in the Lord always. I will say it again: Rejoice! Do not
be anxious about anything, but in every situation, by prayer and
petition, with thanksgiving, present your requests to God. And the
peace of God, which transcends all understanding, will guard your
hearts and your minds in Christ Jesus. "*Philippians 4:4, 6-7 NIV

Such prayer with praise quenches doubts and fears and causes faith to
arise.

SECTION 2

HOW CAN WE HAVE PEACE WITHIN OURSELVES

"So then, make it your top priority to live a life of peace with harmony in your relationships, eagerly seeking to strengthen and encourage one another."

Romans 14:19

Chapter 2:1
Changing How We Think and Behave

> *"If we confess our sins, He is faithful and just to forgive us our sins and to cleanse us from all unrighteousness."* 1 John 1:9

In the Old Testament, the Hebrew word for repentance was sometimes translated as "turn" or "turn around." Its thrust was legal.

> *"Repent! Turn from your idols and renounce all your detestable practices!"* Ezekiel 14:6; 18:30

The word, "return" is also used as in Jeremiah 3:22,

> *"Return, faithless people; I will cure you of backsliding."*

In the New Testament, the Greek word for repentance implied a change of mind and how we think. If we put the meaning of the Hebrew and Greek words together, we get a fuller understanding of what repentance means. As was discussed in the previous section, genuine repentance leads to an inner change of heart which brings us peace and produces the fruits of new thinking and behaviour. Peter explained this change in the following way,

> *"And now you must repent and turn back to God so that your sins will be removed, and so that times of refreshing will stream from the Lord's presence."* Acts 3:19 TPT

At the same time as we are released from any spiritual bonds associated with our former sin behaviour, there is a knock-on effect for good on our families because often spiritual bonds affecting them also become loosed.[74] Thus, when any of us receives healing, there is often far more taking place than we are aware of.

As we read and learn how Jesus related to people, we find that He declared and demonstrated an open heaven,

"for the Kingdom of Heaven is near." Matthew 4:17

Repentance was a response to blessing offered. It was a turning away from and receiving. In his book, Guy Chevreu[x] challenges us to re-think what the gospel call to "repent and believe" is saying. Rather than see this phrase as focusing on the depravity of the human condition, he calls us to focus on the grace of God shown in Christ's sacrifice, the sacrifice of love, a love that woos us to repentance. Guy points out that Gospel grace always precedes obedience,

"It is the love of Christ that compels us." 2 Corinthians 5:14

This is evident in the Gospels, where Jesus healed before demanding a turning away from sin. However, since sin can sometimes, although not always, cause sickness, He entreated those who had been in sin to refrain from it in the future[75] lest they become sick again. Sometimes we need to acknowledge sin and repent before we can receive healing. Although this is not a legality as far as God is concerned, it may be a necessary step for us so that any internal barriers to God that we have constructed in the light of our sin may be removed, and so that we can resist the enemy's taunts.

In turning to Jesus, we can only receive the fullness of the promises that He is making in so far as we are willing to turn away from everything

74 Matthew 18:18.
75 Mark 2:1-12.

that is incompatible with the life He is offering. This includes rejecting sinful or false thinking such as pride, self-rejection, critical thoughts, judgements and un-forgiveness. It includes turning away from sinful deeds and feelings such as immorality, stealing, gossip and aggressive behaviour, and from reactive sins such as anger, hate, bitterness and revenge-seeking. Sin in our lives may affect other areas in our lives and give rise to mental, emotional, physical and social problems.

Love is the key, and anything we do that is not loving is sin. Our model is Jesus, who, while on earth, demonstrated how to live a life of love. The word "agápē" in Greek, translated as "love," is constructed from two words, 'ago' meaning "to lead like a shepherd" and 'páō' meaning "to rest." In the footnote to his translation[xi] of Psalm 23, Brian Simmons writes, "Love is our Shepherd leading us to the place of rest in His heart." It is this kind of love that woos us into repentance for sin and restores peace in our hearts.[76] Understanding this is key to our readily being able to accept that we are forgiven completely. If we have an inner fear that we can never please God, we will find it difficult to believe that we are forgiven, and when reading the Bible, may "tune in" to the wrath of God while forgetting His mercy. It is as though we read the words of life through the lens of death. This can happen by taking a verse out of context or reading only part of a verse and feeling condemned. An example would be reading only the first part of 1 Corinthians 4:5,

"He will bring light to what is hidden in the darkness and will expose the motives of men's hearts."

However, if we read the whole verse, we discover another sentence that totally reverses our previous understanding,

"At that time each will receive his praise from God."

---

76 Romans 2:4; 2 Peter 3:9.

As we read and ponder the Word of God, our heart belief in who God is and what He is like will gradually align with the truth, and we will know the unconditional love of God in our hearts that assures us of the forgiveness offered. God tells us,

> *"For I will forgive their wickedness and will remember their sins no more."* Hebrews 8:12

Where we have a true appreciation of the love, compassion, and forgiveness of God, we are enabled to see through His eyes and to let go of self-condemnation and self-deprecation. We, in turn, can then be more compassionate towards others.

There are two aspects to the process of healing from the effects of sin. These are repentance and cleansing. In his Epistle, John writes,

> *"If we confess our sins, he is faithful and just and will forgive us our sins and purify us from all unrighteousness."* 1 John 1:9

A person may know that their sin is forgiven but still struggle to believe this in their heart if they have not been cleansed from the effects of it. Cleansing may include prayers that break the effects and ongoing influences of self-curses or evil spirits.[77]

We recall how, at the Sea of Tiberias after His resurrection, Jesus helped Peter to feel accepted again.[78] Jesus had already met the disciples twice, but it was the third meeting before He addressed the deep inner guilt and fear that plagued Peter,

> *"Jesus said to Simon Peter, 'Simon, son of Jonah, do you love (agapaō) Me more than these?" He said to Him, 'Yes, Lord; You know that I love (phileō) You'. He said to him, 'Feed My lambs'. He said to him again a second time, 'Simon, son of Jonah, do you love (agapaō) Me?'*

---

77 See The Ministry of the Father's Heart, Book 2, chapter 2.3
78 John 21:17.

He said to Him, 'Yes, Lord; You know that I love (phileō) You'. Jesus said to him, 'Tend My sheep'. He said to him the third time, 'Simon, son of Jonah, do you love (phileō) Me?' Peter was grieved because He said to him a third time 'Do you love (phileō) Me? And he said to Him, "Lord, You know all things; You know that I love (phileō) You." John 21:15-17 NKJV

As Jesus pursued His goal of affirming Peter's love for Him, He stepped down to where Peter was comfortable in his expression of love, using the word, "phileō" rather than the word, "agapaō". He was helping Peter to receive restoration deep into his heart, and to know that he was commissioned to continue the work of shepherding His sheep. What a wonderful, merciful and gracious God we have as our Father. Paul Baloche identifies this love in the lyrics of his song...

Your Mercy[xii]

I once was lost I walked away
The road was dark I could not see
My hope was gone the pain was real
But Your mercy

You saw my steps You felt my fears
You heard my cries You caught my tears
Arms open wide You ran to me
With Your mercy

Your mercy, Your mercy
I stand before my king
And bow my heart to sing
You save me, you raise me
You died so I could live
No greater love than this
Your mercy

You gave me life beyond the grave
My deepest shame is cast away
You sing a song that covers me
It's Your mercy

Your mercy, Your mercy….

Your loving-kindness
It leads me to repentance
Your loving-kindness
It leads me to repentance

Lord let Your kindness
Lead us to repentance
Lord let Your kindness
Lead us to repentance

Your mercy, Your mercy….

In Matthew 5, Jesus says that He has come, not to abolish the law, but to fulfil the law. He stresses the importance of understanding that what goes on in the heart indicates the presence of lawlessness just as much as outward actions. He taught that anyone who is angry with a brother is subject to judgement. Anyone who looks at a woman lustfully has already committed adultery in his heart. As well as urging us to refrain from sexual immorality, impurity and debauchery, idolatry and witchcraft, Paul urges all to refrain from sin in the mind and heart, from hatred, discord, jealousy, fits of rage, selfish ambition, dissensions, factions and envy.[79] It is extremely important that we don't judge others. God does not condemn us and we should not even entertain doing so with others. There is a severe warning for us all in Scripture,

"For in the way you judge, you will be judged; and by your standard of measure, it will be measured to you." Matthew 7:2 NASB

---

79 Galatians 5:19–21.

However, although God instructs us not to judge, He does tell us to discern by His Spirit. Scripture instructs us to pray,

"Teach me good discernment and knowledge for I believe Your commandments." Psalm 119:66

Then to be like Solomon, asking for,

"Instruction in wise behaviour, righteousness, justice and equity." Proverbs 1:1-3

How do we know whether we are judging or discerning? When we judge, we stand on a higher moral ground than the one judged. When we discern, we fall on our knees to pray for them. We are encouraged to live by the Spirit, producing fruit that is Godly,

"But the fruit of the Spirit is love, joy, peace, patience, kindness, goodness, faithfulness, gentleness and self-control. Against such things there is no law." Galatians 5:22-23

Sin within a person and sin against a person can each make a person sick. This was understood by the people when, as recorded in John 9: 1, they asked Jesus, *"Who sinned, this man or his parents, that he was born blind?"* However, Jesus' reply shows us that not all sickness is caused by sin. We must not jump to conclusions, but seek the Holy Spirit for insight. Since sin, (our own or others) may contribute to sickness and oppression, repentance and forgiveness are often important keys to healing and restoration.

Steps in Repentance
Repentance is not an emotion. It is a decision and springs from the will. We agree with God that sin is sin. Let us not use words to absolve ourselves of responsibility. For example, adultery is not just "an affair." As an act of will, we choose to turn away from the sin, renouncing

any negative characteristics of the sin, and confessing it to God, and then cut ourselves free from any bondages associated with the sin,[80] forgiving anyone involved in its origin. We then receive forgiveness and cleansing.[81] Cleansing may include choosing to change a thought pattern or behaviour, and then asking Jesus to surface and take away any associated sinful emotion, together with release from any evil spirit that has become involved.[82] Once we have turned around onto God's path of holy living, we move on, leaving any lingering negative thoughts about the sin behind. Through such a process, our relationship with God is restored, and we have peace with Him and within ourselves. Receiving such healing in our spirits leads to healing from sin-related sicknesses.

---

80 See The Ministry of The Father's Heart, Book 2, Chapter 2.3.
81 1 John 1:9.
82 See The Ministry of The Father's Heart, Book 2, Chapter 2.3.

Chapter 2:2

Resolving the Internal Battle in our Minds and Hearts

"So, I find this law at work: Although I want to do good, evil is right there with me. For in my inner being I delight in God's law; but I see another law at work in me, waging war against the law of my mind and making me a prisoner of the law of sin at work within me."
Romans 7:21-23

In "Why Jesus and the Cross", chapter 1.3, we thought about the amazing transformation that takes place in our spirits by grace through faith when we are born again, and we reflected on how this faith grows in our hearts through meditating on the Word of God. However, because our souls and bodies are not immediately changed by the new birth, much of our former way of thinking, believing and behaving remains and gives rise to an internal battle between what we believe in our spirits and what we think or believe in our souls. Paul describes it in this way,

"For what I do is not the good I want to do; no, the evil I do not want to do—this I keep on doing. Now if I do what I do not want to do, it is no longer I who do it, but it is sin living in me that does it." Romans 7:19-20

Because we see ourselves as not behaving in the way that God would want, we often condemn ourselves and reinforce our former beliefs of being unworthy. Although our worth now comes from Jesus because we are clothed in His righteousness, our learned way of thinking about ourselves, thinking that belongs in our souls, conflicts with the truth that we know in our spirits and from God's Word, and we have an internal battle, sometimes believing one thing, sometimes another. Inner conflict between the old and the new affects our beliefs about and trust in God and His promises. In order to protect ourselves, we may become defensive in our attitudes and actions and these wrong attitudes can affect our health.

The Psalmist writes,

> *"He wore cursing as his garment; it entered into his body like water, into his bones like oil."* Psalm 109:18

There is the suggestion here that what we wear in terms of attitudes and motives, negativity, criticism, and judgement, seeps into our innermost being. This confirms that what we think and feel can have adverse effects on us physically.

Not all beliefs in our hearts are there because of us. Some of our beliefs are inherited because we come from a fallen race. Others have become rooted in our hearts because of circumstances and experiences, or have come from those who have had authority in our lives. Still others are there because of what we have chosen to study and believe. We may not be aware of many until an inner conflict with God's Word brings us revelation.

In his letter to the church in Rome, Paul writes,

> *"Do not conform to the pattern of this world, but be transformed by the renewing of your mind. Then you will be able to test and approve what God's will is - his good, pleasing and perfect will."* Romans 12:2

He also exhorts the church in Corinth to,

"Demolish arguments and every pretension that sets itself up against the knowledge of God, and (we) take captive every thought to make it obedient to Christ." 2 Corinthians 10:5

From such passages, we learn that we have the responsibility to change our thinking, but we know all too well that this is more difficult than it sounds. Attempts to improve our thinking and beliefs do not come by focussing on what we need to stop thinking or believing. If we try this, we will find that it doesn't work for long. We all need God's help, called grace, to enable our minds and hearts to flow in unison with our spirits. The good news is that Jesus within gives us grace to help us in this task. Paul writes about this grace in his letter to the church in Ephesus where he says,

"For it is by grace you have been saved, through faith - and this is not from yourselves, it is the gift of God - not by works, so that no one can boast." Ephesians 2:8-9

This verse is often used to refer to our being born again, but it is a truth that is appropriate to every step in our ongoing salvation, in this case in relation to transformation in our minds and hearts.

We will now consider our own negative and twisted thinking, and our inner vows, both of which may lead us on the pathway of death and despondency. In the next chapter, we will discuss how we can recover from the wounds inflicted on us by others. Selwyn Hughes and Trevor Partridge make this interesting statement;

"We are not so free or independent in our thinking as we might like to think. Every culture makes an indelible impression on its people. The moulding process that begins at birth continues thereafter so that every person is the product of the society in which they live. The human mind is not free even at birth - our

minds have been spiritually hijacked. The Bible puts it strongly
- we are born in sin and shaped in iniquity."[xiii]

David recognises that he was sinful from conception and calls on God
to cleanse and purify him,

*"Have mercy on me, O God, according to your unfailing love;
according to your great compassion blot out my transgressions. Wash
away all my iniquity and cleanse me from my sin. For I know my
transgressions, and my sin is always before me. Against you, you only,
have I sinned and done what is evil in your sight; so, you are right
in your verdict and justified when you judge. Surely, I was sinful at
birth, sinful from the time my mother conceived me. Yet you desired
faithfulness even in the womb; you taught me wisdom in that secret
place. Cleanse me with hyssop, and I will be clean; wash me, and I
will be whiter than snow. Let me hear joy and gladness; let the bones
you have crushed rejoice. Hide your face from my sins and blot out
all my iniquity."* Psalm 51:8-9 NIV

*"Create in me a pure heart, O God, and renew a steadfast spirit
within me."* Psalm 51:10

Renewing a steadfast spirit speaks about strengthening what David
already knew in his spirit, and purifying his heart refers to the flesh part
of him that needed transformation through the grace of God. This is
confirmed by the Jubilee Bible 2000 Translation,

*"Behold, thou dost desire truth in the inward parts, and in the secret
things thou hast made me to know wisdom."*

I believe these Scriptures point to the wisdom which is restored at our
rebirth and that is one of the attributes in our spirits with which we are
created because we are made in the image of God,

"But there is a spirit in man: and the inspiration of the Almighty..."
Job 32:8

We are invited to ask God for wisdom,

"If any of you lacks wisdom, he should ask God, who gives generously to all without finding fault, and it will be given to him." James 1:5

"For the LORD gives wisdom; From His mouth come knowledge and understanding." Proverbs 2:6

God has given us His Holy Spirit within our spirits, thereby renewing our spirits as a means of guiding us in the work of transforming our minds and hearts through co-operating with His grace.

We are continuously processing thoughts, sometimes without being consciously aware of it. Many different thoughts such as football results, anxieties and work schedules can buzz in and out of our heads. Though largely unnoticed, we talk to ourselves at anything up to 1300 words per minute. Thoughts that jump into our minds without any conscious effort can be the result of past influences, events and experiences or from the enemy. Some thoughts play repeatedly like tapes, just below the level of the subconscious, and greatly influence us. The enemy has a profound influence on some of these tapes, with his main strategy being to push us into thinking independently of God. This often results in a sense of hopelessness in the face of difficulties. The things that bring us to the edge of depression, that make problems seem insurmountable, or that affect relationships adversely, are often the things that we are telling ourselves. Paul urges us to renew our minds[83] and, in his letter to the Ephesians, he writes,

"Now your attitudes and thoughts must all be constantly changing for the better." Ephesians 4:23 TLB

---

83 Romans 12:2.

Our emotions, a bit like the warning light on a car indicating that all is not well, can be like warning lights that something is wrong and needs sorting. Our emotions come from our thinking, whether it is conscious, subconscious or unconscious thinking. Sometimes when an event has been so traumatic that it has become buried in the subconscious or unconscious parts of our mind, it may seem that it has disappeared forever; but those thoughts and negative emotions associated with the event influence our present thinking, feelings, and decision making.

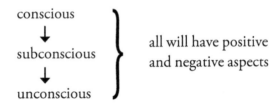

conscious
↓
subconscious
↓
unconscious

all will have positive
and negative aspects

Many good habits operate from the subconscious e.g., changing gear in a car. At first, changing gear requires concentration, but eventually, it becomes second nature and operates from the subconscious. Equally, we may be aware of some thoughts, good and bad, that operate from our subconscious e.g., good words that encourage others or good decisions that help others, but also bad thoughts about ourselves which make us feel miserable or reveal our jealousy of others. The negative ones can have a harmful knock-on effect on our lives.

We might wonder how our thoughts along with associated emotions can become stored in our subconscious or unconscious mind. This can happen for many reasons, perhaps as a consequence of trauma, or because of repetition or denial. In the third book of this series we will be taking an in-depth look at what can happen in our spirits and souls as a result of trauma and how our hearts can be affected. For now, we will focus on how we dispose of those highly-charged wrong perceptions or wrong conclusions and subsequent self-talk of which we are aware.

If the pain from some relationship or experience threatens us in some way that affects our sense of self-worth, we may conclude, "I am no good; I can never do anything right; it's all my fault." God wants us to face such thoughts with Him so that He can show us the truth through His Word, and He wants us to learn to practise the following,

> *"Whatever is true, whatever is noble, whatever is right, whatever is pure, whatever is lovely, whatever is admirable—if anything is excellent or praiseworthy—think about such things."* Philippians 4:8

When we live in this way, not allowing negativity to become rooted, then we will cease to have our focus on ourselves and be able to encourage and build others up spontaneously. However, very few of us are disciplined in this way and so, in order to cope despite having a poor self-image, we may repress such thinking by repeatedly pushing it to the back of our minds until it becomes stored in our subconscious mind. Once the pain is stored away, the person's subconscious goes into active duty, gathering all kinds of verifying evidence that seem to affirm the negativity. Then, although we may not be aware of it, the negative patterns of thinking are in control, working against us, and we react negatively inwardly, outwardly, or upwardly, condemning ourselves, blaming, criticizing, and resenting others, or turning against God. We may find it difficult to trust anyone, including God. We may excuse such behaviour by exclaiming, "that's just how I am," but that excuse does not address the root of the problem.

As adults, many of these wrong attitudes, perceptions and habits have become our variety of flesh pattern that is buried deep within, and our tendency is,

> *"To walk according to the flesh instead of according to the Spirit."*
> Romans 8:4 NASB

Walking according to the flesh causes blockages that keep us from experiencing freedom within ourselves and in our relationships with God and with others.

If we are going to be able to address this, we must, first of all, become aware of what has happened or is happening, and of what is twisted or negative in our thinking, whether it is fear of authority, feelings of insignificance, or a belief that we are boring. Sometimes because of negative or twisted thinking, we can make inner vows such as, "I must never....," "I will not...." It can be difficult to recognise such negative thinking in ourselves, but God will help us when we ask Him. As we open our hearts to Him and invite the Holy Spirit to search them we can expect to be made aware of anything that needs changed,

> "Search me, O God, and know my heart; test me and know my anxious thoughts. See if there is any offensive way in me, and lead me in the way everlasting." Psalm139:23-24

Through inviting Jesus into our exploration, we know that as we respond to His gentle conviction that He will breathe His life through our minds and hearts. We can ask ourselves questions like, "What am I thinking or saying to myself?" Or, "Is what I'm thinking truth, as laid out in Scripture?" "Is my self-talk healthy or unhealthy?" "Are these helpful or harmful conclusions?" Sometimes as we listen to others, we may recognise in ourselves, attitudes similar to those with which they struggle. In response, we can choose to take responsibility for our thoughts, attitudes and behaviour by coming humbly before God in acknowledgement. Sometimes it helps to be willing to share our feelings, doubts, and sins with a safe person.[84]

As we take a responsibility for thoughts, we can replace negative self-talk with the truth according to Scripture. It is up to each one of us to choose life and not death. In Deuteronomy 30: 19-20a we read,

---

84 James 5:16.

"This day I call heaven and earth as witnesses against you that I [God] have set before you life and death, blessing and curses. Now choose life, so that you and your children may live and that you may love the Lord your God, listen to His voice, and hold fast to Him."

There is a clear link here between blessing and life, and between cursing and death. Our own words, and the words of others, can bring blessing or curse, life or death.[85] Every thought influences the cells in our bodies for good or ill. As Scriptures tell us,

"The tongue has the power of life or death." Proverbs 18:21

"Pleasant words are a honeycomb, sweet to the soul and healing to the bone." Proverbs 16:24

Above all, God gives us His grace to enable us to change,

"I know that you delight to set your truth deep in my spirit. So now come into the hidden places of my heart and teach me wisdom." Psalm 51:6 TPT

In this fight to align our thinking with the Word of God, we must remember that we are the righteousness of Christ and that this was never, and cannot ever, be earned. The truths in God's Word that tell us who we are, refer to the righteousness that became ours at rebirth and are aspects of who we are as spirit beings. Even though we see evidence to the contrary in our lives, any unrighteous thoughts and beliefs come from a part of us that is still in the process of being transformed into the likeness of Christ.

---

85 Proverbs 12:18 GW.

Some wrong thinking and flesh patterns:

o   "All or nothing" - we think that failure in one thing means
    that we're a failure in everything.
o   Perfectionism in relationships e.g., the belief that people
    can only love us if we do what they want all the time.
o   Perfectionism in tasks. This is unrealistic. Our goals must
    be realistic and reachable.
o   Self-rejection. We need to recognise negative thinking that
    can be changed, and learn not to transfer it into negativity
    about who we are.
o   Competing for recognition.
o   Truth out of balance, e.g., denying ourselves to the point
    of never considering our own needs.
o   Inability to reconcile good and bad, e.g., seeing someone
    or something as all good or all bad.
o   Clinging to someone who affirms us.
o   Becoming a people-pleaser.
o   Withdrawing into ourselves.
o   Wearing a mask.
o   Venting anger all around us.
o   Blame shifting.
o   Gaining acceptance through becoming a rescuer.
o   Becoming legalistic.
o   Entering into denial.
o   Using control, whether consciously or subconsciously.

We can have distorted views of ourselves, of others, of God, and our
Christian lives. We may struggle with unhealthy shame, invalid guilt or
always needing approval. We may be afraid to say, "no" in case someone
rejects us, or we may have blurred boundaries and set no limits as to
what others can expect of us. We may think that God doesn't want us to
have our wishes or desires or that He wants us to have everything that we
want and pray for. We may think that God wants us to submit to others

regardless of how they treat us. We can think it's not biblical to think of our own needs, that our problems are the cause of sin in our lives. On the other hand, we may believe that others are responsible for us.

There is good and there is evil in the world. There is pain, sin, and suffering. People are a mix of good and bad and God loves us all. He says we are incredibly wonderful, created in the image of God, and overflowing with all sorts of talents, even though we may be sinful and broken and beset with all sorts of weaknesses. When we read about the woman caught in adultery, we see that Jesus accepted her with loving compassion and at the same time told her she needed to do something about the bad part.

We can change any destructive patterns in our lives with God's help as we come before Him in humility and with a readiness to acknowledge that we have a problem. As we ask the Holy Spirit to reveal any wrong motives, beliefs, prejudices, etc. that are hidden in our hearts,[86] we can identify any pattern of ungodly thinking or behaviour that we have and He will bring the truths of Scripture to our minds so that we can receive them, thus transforming our minds to the mind of Christ. Within this process, if any hurtful emotions surface, we can ask Jesus to take them away and give us His peace. As we persevere the changes will take place.

Reflection
Think of some examples of negative or twisted thinking. What are some of the thought patterns that you might find yourself repeating almost subconsciously? Can you think of any inner vows that you have made? Talk to God about them and ask Him to help you to change.

Further insight from Ellis's ABC theory of emotions[xiv] may help us in our exploration. We might think that it is events that produce consequences and that it is an event that causes our feelings or emotions, but really it is our belief or self-talk about the event that determines what we feel about it. To change our feelings, we don't have to change the event (which we

---

86 Psalm 130:23-24.

cannot) but we do need to change how we interpret and talk to ourselves about the event. God tells us that our thoughts create our emotions,

"For as he thinks in his heart so is he." Proverbs 23:7 NKJ

So often we brood over perceived hardships rather than seeking the face of God to receive His peace,

"You will keep him in perfect peace whose mind is stayed on you." Isaiah 16:3

We need to take responsibility for our own emotional life and not be a victim of the negative events in our lives.

God is the one who can help us in this matter. First, we have to choose to deal with it. This is a choice that isn't a choice if we want to be free. But, then, having chosen to be free, we may seek God's help. Change may occur instantly through His sovereign grace, or it may take place over time, often through meditating on God's Word and allowing it to penetrate deeply. Change, effected with God's help, is deep and lasting and goes to the core of the issue. Otherwise, we may continue to battle over deeply ingrained and reactive emotions for a very long time. It is interesting for us to read an example of the detrimental effect of negative self-talk as recorded in Numbers 13:1-14:10, the account of the twelve who were sent to explore the land of Canaan. The self-talk of the ten led to their exclusion from the Promised Land, whereas the self-talk of Joshua and Caleb led to an exciting and fulfilling future there. In a similar way, our self-talk will either facilitate a future full of hope or one in which we struggle in despair.

God doesn't do anything wrong. His plans are never to harm us but always to give us a future and a hope.[87] When we are faced with seemingly disastrous events, we may think that what He allows is

---

87 Jeremiah 29:11.

inconsistent with our beliefs of how a loving God would act, but He has chosen not to overrule the choices we make in life and has handed over to us all the authority we need to overcome the work of the evil one. Our responses to life experiences are important. Having heart surrender to and confident trust in God, and continuing to worship Him,[88] allows Him to act on our behalf. Then we will recognise that it is not so much the nature of the event that matters as our self-talk, our interpretation of the event, and our response.

Sometimes we can recognise the wrong attitude or action before we understand the emotion driving it. For example we may recognise within ourselves a persistent need to control without knowing why but when we seek insight through the Holy Spirit we may discover that we have an unconsciously held mindset that says, "I must take control and do what I can to get and keep my world in order." Sometimes such control is a learned pattern, but it can be a response to some event which was outside our control and which provoked extreme fear. Subsequently, tremendous fear can come upon such a person if they feel they are out of control, and so as an adult, they may try to control others.

Over time, if we regularly feed our minds with the truth in Scripture while relying on the grace of God and the promptings of the Holy Spirit, we will find our emotions becoming healthy and life-giving.[89] God loves and cares for us and has promised to work everything together for the good of those who love Him and have been called according to His purpose.[90]

Previously, we talked about the fact that our hearts are like control centres in our lives. What we believe in our hearts dictates direction, and, if not aligned with the truth, will cause doubts and fears to take the place of confident truth in God. There are many reasons as to why we have the heart beliefs that we have, some inherited and some developed throughout life.

---

88 Job 1:21.
89 Zechariah 4:6.
90 Romans 8:28.

Four of the reasons why unbelief or doubt may be in our hearts are:

Ignorance
If we do not know what God has said then we are not positioned to have faith according to what His Word says. For example, if we don't know that God has promised to be near us all the time, then we will not live our lives trusting Him to be near.

Misbelief
If we have been taught wrongly or influenced in an unbiblical way in what we believe, then our mindsets, hearts beliefs and attitudes will not allow us to move with the faith given to us and we may have a divided heart. If we are independent and self-sufficient, we may take our logical, deductive, observational thinking into the Kingdom of God, letting it take precedence over God's wisdom, and then wonder why faith doesn't work. Reason and intellect have their place in helping us make decisions, but they should not dictate to the spiritual realm. If we are afraid, we may resort to our own strategies as, for example, Abraham who became frightened for his safety when in Egypt and passed Sarah off as his sister. What did he do when the deception was discovered? He returned to the place where he had last trusted God and started his life of faith again. If we find that we have shifted from trusting God to trusting in ourselves, we may feel that we've blown it, condemn ourselves, and feel like giving up, but God wants to help us, and so we can repent, turn around and retrace our steps to the point of departure from trust in God, and move forward once again with Him. When we abide in Jesus and allow His Word to cleanse us and to help us in pulling down strongholds - that is, imaginations and every high thought that sets itself up against Jesus[91] - we discover that His truth transforms misbelief into trust.

A Hardened Heart
This may happen because of pride, for example, pride in our own wisdom, or perhaps because of the self-protection that arises after

---
91 2 Corinthians 19:4-5.

disappointment, hurt, scepticism or other people's influential words. Anything that causes a hardened heart will in some way prevent us from being sensitive towards miracles and healings or any grace blessing. Anything negative that we dwell upon in our minds affects our hearts adversely. When, instead, we think about the Lord who loves us and whom we love, and about His goodness and kindness, we become sensitive, and open, to all He wants to give us.

Misguided Beliefs
Those which arise from the senses - what we see, hear, feel, smell or touch - can adversely influence us into opposing what faith reveals. We need to set these aside and believe what the Spirit is saying,

"And not being weak in faith, he did not consider his own body, already dead (since he was about a hundred years old), and the deadness of Sarah's womb. He did not waver at the promise of God through unbelief but was strengthened in faith, giving glory to God and being fully convinced of what He had promised He was also able to perform." Romans 4:19 NKJV

Some years ago while praying, I sensed some words arising from my spirit and knew that they were from God,

"Invest in My Nature."

As I thought about what this might mean I realised that God was asking me to allow His nature, which is in my spirit, to influence my soul.

This was followed by further words, again rising up from my spirit,

"Murder my animal instincts."

I was horrified. I was puzzled. Did I really have animal instincts? Why did the words seem to come from me? It was some time before I was able to understand and accept this instruction. The presence of the Holy Spirit within me had convicted me in my spirit that I needed to resolve flesh issues in my soul. However, I was not being left on my own to sort this as I then sensed words that clarified the way forward for me,

"Water my soul."

I knew that God was showing me that as I invested in His nature, which is present in my spirit, and watered my soul with the Word of God, I would find that my animal instincts which are a part of my fallen nature and in my soul, would be "murdered."

Our heart beliefs will align with the truth of God's Word as we read and meditate on the Word of God and speak truth. Not only does my faith tell me to believe God when something in the natural realm appears to contradict what I believe He is saying, but it also requires me to trust without seeing the end result. God commends all faith and, in the gospels, we read how Jesus often did likewise.

Chapter 2:3

Forgiving Ourselves and Others

"Never hold a grudge or try to get even, but plan your life around the noblest way to benefit others. Do your best to live as everybody's friend."
Romans 12:17-18 TPT

Not only does hurt inflicted cause turmoil in our thinking and emotions, but there is no doubt that this subsequent "dis-ease" can affect our bodies adversely, possibly with disease. In Psalm 38:7, the psalmist writes,

"My loins are full of inflammation, and there is no soundness in my flesh." NKJV

"A raging fever burns within me, and my health is broken." NLT

In response to a distressing vision in which revelation is given about a time when betrayal, looting and attack will come against Babylon, Isaiah writes,

"at this my body is racked with pain, ... " Isaiah 21:3

Daniel and Nahum recorded the effect of fear and anguish on people's bodies,

"His face turned pale and he was so frightened that his knees knocked together and his legs gave way." Daniel 5:6

"Hearts melt, knees give way, bodies tremble, every face grows pale."
Nahum 2:10

Ezekiel writes about groaning with a broken heart and bitter grief. Medical experts tell us that continued dis-ease, like anguish and anxiety, can lead to physical ailments like bowel disease, heart trouble and stomach ulcers. Emotions like fear and anger can take up residence in the seat of our emotions, our loins, sometimes causing back trouble.

What are some of the symptoms of unforgiveness in our hearts?
Perhaps we are replaying some event in our minds or having internal conversations in which we come out on top,

"Do not gloat when your enemy falls; when he stumbles, do not let your heart rejoice." Proverbs 24:17

Perhaps we even feel self-righteous about the offence against us or think of the person with whom we are in conflict as totally bad. Another sign that a hurt is lingering occurs when we try to avoid being in the person's company, or when seeing them results in a physical reaction such as shortness of breath or fear, or when we want something to take the person out of our life. We may recognise it by realising that an emotion that we are feeling is totally out of proportion to an event. Paul provides the answer,

"Who will rescue me from this body of death? Thanks be to God- through Jesus Christ our Lord!" Romans 7:24a-25

Have we a part to play in the transformation? Yes, we do. There are decisions to be made as well as grace to be received.

Decisions to be made
When we believe the truths about who we are in Christ and that our lives are safe in His hands, we are enabled to stand unwavering and to

feel secure even in the face of criticism and condemnation, anger and negativity, or hurtful words and actions. When we know that God loves us and knows all that is happening in our lives, we can trust Him to help us to resolve everything through the transforming power of Jesus,

"Behold the eye of the Lord is upon them that fear Him, upon them that hope in His mercy." Psalm 33:18 KJV

"All the paths of the Lord are mercy and truth unto such as keep His covenant and His testimonies." Psalm 25:10 KJV

"He has showed you, O Man, what is good. And what does the Lord require of you? To act justly and to love mercy and to walk humbly with your God." Micah 6:8

This means that we will be able to assess honestly and without fear, whether we have been in the wrong or not, and to accept responsibility without feeling rejected and a failure. Equally, with God's help and in a way that offers love and not hate, we will be able to work through pain, fear, and the hurt inflicted on us,

"But I say to you who hear: Love your enemies, do good to those who hate you, bless those who curse you, and pray for those who spitefully use you.... But love your enemies, do good and lend, hoping for nothing in return: and your reward will be great, and you will be sons of the Most High. For He is kind to the unthankful and evil." Luke 6:27-35

If however, we react in an angry spirit and try to vindicate ourselves, we hinder God from being free to work in us and in the other person, and God leaves us to sort it out in our own way. In Jesus' story about the unmerciful servant, we are told that the master said to the unforgiving servant, "Shouldn't you have had mercy on your fellow servant just as I had on you?" and that he turned him over to the jailors (his tormentors)

until he should pay back what he owed.[92] In the New King James
Version, we read that he was delivered up to the *"torturers."* When we
refuse to show mercy towards others, we subject ourselves to torturers;
emotions like bitterness, anger, hatred or fear. We lose our peace and
no longer have freedom. We have taken the law into our own hands
and are carrying out the judgement ourselves. We imprison ourselves
and imprison the offender. Why help the devil in his work of making
people captives? Paul writes,

> *"Do not take revenge, my friends, but leave room for God's wrath,*
> *for it is written 'It is mine to avenge; I will repay,' says the Lord. How*
> *the Lord chooses to sort things out is not our concern. He will come*
> *to that person with the same loving offer of forgiveness and mercy as*
> *that with which He comes to us."* Romans 12:19

We are urged to take responsibility for what goes on in our minds. Paul
writes that we are to,

> *"take captive every thought to make it obedient to Christ."*
> 2 Corinthians 10:5

Our minds then become transformed and aligned to the mind of Christ.
If we hold on to angry thoughts and feelings about what has happened
to hurt us, we may end up pushing them down inside and then find,
that over the years, deep within, we have developed a boiling cauldron
of venom, perhaps anger, bitterness or resentment. We may find we
can no longer control the anger, but that the anger controls us and has
made us prisoners. Paul describes this as,

> *"giving the devil a foothold."* Ephesians 4:27

If we then seek to forgive, this deep-seated spirit of anger may rise within
us and make that difficult. The anger which we have used to defend

92 Matthew 18:33-34.

ourselves has become part of our clothing and imprisoned us. If we give our hearts to evil, evil can have an influence over us. If it has become deeply rooted then deliverance may be helpful.[93] Sometimes, over the long term, our bodies may suffer because of the internal turmoil and become sick.

If, rather than react to hurts and offences, we respond in the Spirit of Jesus, blessing rather than cursing, we give God freedom to do what He knows is best.

> *"But you must return to your God; maintain love and justice and wait for your God always."* Hosea 12: 6 KJV

He wants to bless and be merciful to us all. As we forgive and invite Him into our hurt, asking Him to remove it, we can be sure that He will, and we will be able to join with the Psalmist in his words of thanksgiving to God,

> *"I will sing of Your love and justice; to You, O Lord, I will sing praise."* Psalm 101:1

The writer of Proverbs 16:6 offers us some good advice on the subject,

> *"Through love and faithfulness sin is atoned for: through the fear of the Lord a man avoids evil."*

Mike Bickle writes; "When we are kind to our enemies, we mirror the Father's kindness for evil and ungrateful men, and we come into unity with the Ruler of the Universe. There is no form of spiritual warfare more powerful than that."[xv]

We will be able to rejoice in the amazing grace extended to us as children of God with all that that means in terms of blessing for us, but also

---

93 Book 2 in the series, The Ministry of the Father's Heart.

blessing through us to others. And as we allow this truth to shape us, we will no longer feel like orphans, misfits, or outsiders, but will be able to celebrate belonging with our brothers and sisters to the family of God, where we are all on an equal footing, each special, each of value, each important, each a vessel of the love of God to others.

Even when we are justified in being angry, for example when we are betrayed, what starts as a reasonable reaction to an offence, may turn into a life sentence for us if we don't resolve it in God's way. Anger in itself is not necessarily a sin. It is what we do with anger that determines whether we sin. Paul, in his letter to the Ephesians, writes,

"In your anger do not sin." Ephesians 4:26a

The implication is that there will be times when we are angry (emotion) but we are not to work out our anger in sin. Paul continues,

"Do not let the sun go down on your wrath."

We are to recognize what is going on within and not nurse it but do something about it. Knowing that we are loved by God no matter what, and feeling deeply secure in His love, is what helps us to face our shortcomings without devaluing who we are and perhaps turning to protective strategies.

Jesus taught how important forgiveness is. It is a decision of the mind and will. We forgive because in Christ we are forgiven and restored in our relationship with Him.[94] Jesus taught us that we must forgive and He showed that forgiveness is the pathway to receiving healing because it frees us from the tormentors such as bitterness and hatred.[95] Forgiveness releases us from the past, restores the present, and heals us for the future. Nowhere does Scripture say that we are to make people

94 Ephesians 4:32.
95 Matthew 18:21-35.

apologise to us before we forgive them, and nowhere does it say that we have to make them forgive us.

Grace to be received
God says that we are to forgive from the heart. Initially, we may find that we are unable to do so because thoughts of anger, hatred or self-pity seek priority. Try as we might, our hurting emotions keep welling up and we do not feel like forgiving. We can choose to do so, but with gritted teeth and not from the heart. Such a response leaves neither us nor the person who offended free. The better way is to ask God for His help and this comes in different ways.

Even when we are struggling with forgiving there can be an honesty within us that wants things to be different and that is sufficient to allow God in to help us. I have heard where God invited someone to ask Him for His forgiveness and this step enabled that person to forgive. At other times through receiving the grace of God, some are able to choose to forgive as an act of the will, even though they do not feel like doing so. This is only a first step but a big one. As we set our goal in the right direction, we are engaged in the process and can move forward. There may be an outworking in our minds and hearts still to take place, but we are on our way to freedom; a step we can only take through obedience.

When we come to Him for help, we acknowledge the truth about what has taken place but without condemnation in our hearts. Jesus said,

"You will know the truth, and the truth will set you free." John 8:32

Many of us throughout life have learned to hide emotions, to push away pain, rejection, and aggression. In focussing all our resources on pushing down feelings and behaviour that we don't want to admit to, we put on a good front. And therein lies the root problem. On the face of it, we are succeeding, but in trying to resolve issues in our own strength we are denying the truth. Jesus never said, "Pretend things don't hurt or make you angry or fearful." Jesus never said, "Don't be angry. Good Christians are never angry." Jesus wants us to be real. He, Himself, expressed His emotions openly to His Father,

> *"My soul is overwhelmed with sorrow to the point of death. My Father, if it is possible, may this cup be taken from me. Yet not as I will but as You will."* Matthew 26:38-39

As Christians, all too often we forgive as an act of obedience and in a desire to please God, and then immediately move on as though that is the issue dealt with. Later on, when we still feel anger or resentment, we may blame ourselves for not having forgiven properly, and perhaps say the words again. We may do this repeatedly and yet find no peace. Sometimes our forgiveness is genuine but we still struggle. Why is this? It can be because we have never acknowledged our hurt with a view to being released from it through the love of our Father. Unless we allow ourselves to see truth, we cannot be free, and, since most hurtful things are the consequence of sin, this needs to be faced and not covered up with phrases like, "They didn't mean it." Such a statement may well be true, but if we have been hurt, such an excuse sends us into denial about our hurt and will not free us from the pain. When we simply state the truth that the words or action which caused hurt was sin, we don't do it as a judgement but as a truth that will open the floodgates of our emotional pain. As this come to the surface and we release it to Jesus, asking Him to take it away, the consequences of the hurt leave us and inner peace is restored. Such releasing may be unpleasant for a few moments, but a release is important if we are to be free, especially if we are full of fear and panic. Praying in this way while exhaling deeply will allow the fear, panic or other negative emotions to leave, and allow Jesus to replace them with peace. We may also need to talk to Jesus with full awareness of all that we have felt in response to the actions of others. Sometimes our reactions may be sinful, in which case we need to repent. Paul wrote about this to the Colossian church (believers),

"Put off all these: anger, wrath, malice, blasphemy, filthy language out of your mouth... put on tender mercies, kindness, humility, meekness, longsuffering ... but above all these things put on love, which is the bond of perfection. And let the peace of God rule in your hearts." Colossians 3:8, 12, 14-15

Once we have allowed God to work in our hearts, releasing negative emotions and giving us peace, we will usually discover that forgiveness is felt at a heart level and we will not have any continuing negative reactions to the person. If we are still struggling, then we may need to come to Jesus again for deeper release. Forgiveness is often a process. What is important is our willingness to engage in the process and so stay out of a self-made prison.

We know that forgiveness is complete when a person's confession has become unimportant to us and we no longer need to hear it; when we can meet the person without feeling fear or whatever emotion was imprisoning us; when we can think of the person without little scenarios going around and around in our heads, and when we can act like Jesus would in the situation and be able to bless them.

Reflection
You may like to meditate on the actions of both the father and the elder brother in the story of the prodigal son as found in Luke 15:11-32. You could ask God to reveal times to you when you have responded like the father and times when you have been more like the son. He will meet with you, offering mercy. Henri Nouwen writes,[xvi]

The lostness of the resentful 'saint' is so hard to reach precisely because it is so closely wedded to the desire to be good and virtuous. I know how diligently I have tried to be good, acceptable, likeable, and a worthy example for others. There was always the conscious effort to avoid the pitfalls of sin and the constant fear of giving in to temptation. But with all of that there came a seriousness, a moralistic intensity - and even a touch of fanaticism - that made it increasingly difficult to feel at home in my Father's house. I became less free, less spontaneous, less playful, and others came to see me more and more as a somewhat 'heavy' person.

He continues,

When I listen carefully to the words with which the elder son attacks his father - self-righteous, jealous words - I hear a deeper complaint. It is the complaint that comes from a heart that feels it never received what it was due. It is the complaint that cries out: "I tried so hard, worked so long, did so much, and still I have not received what others receive so easily. Why do people not thank me, not invite me, not play with me, not honour me, while they pay so much attention to those who take life so easily and so casually?

In the attitude of the elder son, we recognise a religious spirit, one that seeks to earn acceptance through works rather than through grace and who, therefore, expects reward and praise, and cannot rejoice in the good that comes to others. Praise God, we are people of grace and given every opportunity to be at peace in our relationships with others.

When we forgive someone, it does not mean that we have to go to the person and tell them that we have forgiven them. Nor does it mean we have to enter into the same relationship again immediately, although that can happen. Trust sometimes takes time to build up again between people, but God's desire is always for true reconciliation of heart and mind and restoration of relationships.

Chapter 2:4

Inner (Emotional) Healing

"Come to Me, all you who labour and are heavy laden, and I will give you rest. Take My yoke upon you and learn from Me, for I am gentle and lowly in heart, and you will find rest for your souls. For My yoke is easy and My burden is light." Matthew 11:28-30

Sometimes we can be aware that our emotional responses seem totally out of proportion, perhaps being consumed with extreme anger or being immobilized by fear or inadequacy. Despite meditating on the truth in God's Word, and bringing every thought captive in obedience to Christ, we may still be living anxious and worried lifestyles, or struggling with jealousy, bitterness or resentments, sense a loss of identity or have an inability to trust anyone. We may recognise recurrent thought patterns which we believe such as, "I'm no use", "nobody cares about me", "I'm to blame", which when challenged have no substance to them. We may be plagued with issues such as eating disorders, self-harm, sexual promiscuity or depression. Our response to such apparently unresolvable upheaval may be to develop protective strategies and defence mechanisms or to abdicate responsibility. The intensity of personal problems can be so extreme that, even for the devoted Christian, God can seem to be far away. Central to such inner pain is what we have come to believe in our hearts, which then works its way out into our everyday lives. Through the process of inner healing, our heart beliefs are changed into alignment with those of God, and our sense of significance and security in Christ grows. Our hearts become established in grace and the turmoil ceases. This process of inner healing, sometimes called emotional healing, when undertaken through the guidance of the Holy Spirit, frequently brings the release and relief that people are seeking, and is simply enforcing the victory that Jesus won for us at the cross when,

> *"He was pierced for our transgressions, he was crushed for our iniquities; the punishment that brought us peace was on him, and by his wounds we are healed."* Isaiah 53:5

This journey begins when we are willing and able to acknowledge our need for help. It is advantageous to find someone whom we trust to accompany us on our journey, a journey guiding us into seeing what God wants to show us about our past, and into an understanding of what needs to happen for our healing. This is a journey into the heart of God where we find our true selves; forgiven, cleansed, delivered, and released. This journey is all about meeting with Jesus and walking with Him through life experiences with their accompanying thoughts and emotions.

Through the ministry of the Holy Spirit, God our Father can help us to see what is truly happening and to understand the truth that will set us free in Christ. Being willing to revisit whatever the Spirit recalls to our minds from the past can be frightening, as none of us likes to face hidden things in case they become too painful.

Root causes of this inner turmoil may arise because of generational iniquity, the sin of others or our own sin. They can arise because of life circumstances or originate in times of national stress and distress. In any one person, the reasons can be numerous and interwoven in a complicated manner into the fabric of their life. So, consequently, looking to God in total dependence is necessary as He is the One who can open the way to revelation, understanding and healing. Such a journey requires the person to trust God and be willing to give Him permission to open what has been shut down. Only in this way can what is hidden come into the light and be resolved. Doing this makes the person vulnerable, and so anyone travelling with them must be trustworthy and be willing to offer unconditional love.

It is a step-by-step journey in which we discover first-hand from our Father that He has remained with us throughout our life and has walked with us through the bad times. Although He cannot change our past experiences, He does re-interpret them for us through revelation of His loving presence and, perhaps, some truth that we have overlooked. As His gentle loving voice reaches into our past with truth and grace, it is as though the pain-filled garments of the past fall away and are one by one replaced with garments of peace, love, acceptance, contentment, joy and freedom. We come into a revelation of the deep, deep love and unconditional acceptance of our heavenly Father and we rest in the knowledge that we are totally pure and beautiful in Him. As we receive healing, our defensiveness and need for self-protective mechanisms are dismantled, and we are set free to live in the light.

Sometimes our problems can surface at the time of conversion or at a time of being baptised in the Holy Spirit. For some, these times are accompanied by amazing and instantaneous release, deliverance, and healing but, for many, healing comes more gradually. Jesus has completed all that is necessary for healing at the cross, but, as we have indicated earlier, over our lifetime we continue to work out our salvation in our souls and bodies. God's process of healing us involves us and our choices, as they contribute to the changes that are made in our thought patterns, perceptions, emotional health, and beliefs. It is a process of discipling, helping us through the renewal of our minds and the transforming love of the Father.

In ministry for inner healing or healing of memories, there is a comprehensiveness, a caring for the whole person. Not only is the person healed from pain and hurt from the past but they are discipled to be able to walk with Jesus through the troubles of the future in such a way that, no matter what comes against them, they are equipped with the knowledge and wisdom and loving power of the Spirit to enable them to resolve it. Truly effective healing in Jesus' Name strengthens a person to be an overcomer.

We can find insights into the process for emotional healing by reading Psalm 23, a psalm describing the total care of our Shepherd, Jesus. We know that we, as His sheep, can hear our Shepherd's voice and hear Him call us by name as He leads us to a place of pasture and contentment.[96]

"The Lord is my Shepherd; I shall not be in want. He makes me lie down in green pastures, He leads me beside quiet waters, He restores my soul." Psalm 23:1-3a

The Hebrew word "menuhâ" translated here as, "quiet waters" can also be translated as, "the waters of a resting place".[97]

Inner healing is a gentle, deep, loving and powerful ministry, one in which we encourage the one looking for healing to meet with Jesus and be touched deep within their soul with the truth of His love for them. He does this in a way that lets them know they are special and that He really, really knows them. On one occasion I was praying with a young girl and listening to her story. Throughout our time together, a very strange word kept coming to mind, but I kept pushing it away because I thought it would sound silly to the girl. Eventually, I gave in and asked her whether the word, "ragamuffin" meant anything to her. She immediately brightened up and with a big smile told me that it was her mother's pet name for her. No one else would have known. This was especially meaningful to a girl who felt that her mother didn't love her as, with this one word, Jesus showed her the truth about her mum and that He, too, really knew her. From this, she gained confidence that He

96 John 10:10.
97 Isaiah 11:10.

could help her. He truly is her Shepherd and was leading her to a true place of rest in His heart.

Jesus shows Himself as being present in a loving way within any stressful situation. An example of this arose while ministering to someone who had been deeply traumatised on several occasions throughout life. As usual we did not set the agenda but looked to God to guide us through. Having asked Him to lead us forward in what He wanted to do with the person that day, the Holy Spirit then brought back to her mind a specific event which had taken place when she had been two years old. As I waited quietly, I witnessed a scenario that I have never forgotten. This event had been traumatising for her as a child, and now as an adult, she saw before her eyes a re-enactment of the incident. Painful emotions rose up within her but, simultaneously, in the spirit, she saw something that she had never seen before. Jesus was under the kitchen table, smiling at the little girl and with His finger to His lips, indicating that His presence was a secret known only to her. As she released the overflow of emotional pain that this insight had brought, a deep certainty was established within her that Jesus had known all about what had happened and had been present with her throughout. Consequently, peace and reassurance became rooted in her heart. As always, Jesus used a uniquely beautiful way in which to meet with her in her need.

At other times, a series of pictures given by the Holy Spirit will show the progress being made as Jesus heals a person, sometimes from hurt so painful that they have locked part of themselves away in order to be able to function in the world. Many years ago, while ministering inner healing to a young woman, I was shown a wee child looking forlornly through a fireguard at a lovely warm fire. Her arms were hanging limp, a teddy dangling from her right hand. I asked God to remove the barrier that she had to receiving His love and to draw her close. As I prayed, I saw the child, now on His knee, wrestling to get off. I then prayed for His peace, reassurance, and love to fill the child, and as I continued to observe the picture, I saw the wee one, still on His knee, calm down and go to sleep. The next time we met to pray, I saw that this same child, now sliding down off the Father's knee, was happy and confident as she stood beside Him.

Another time, a lady was being shown why she was so frightened in life. She saw with her spiritual eyes something that had happened when she was eight years old. She had gone along a dark passage to answer what she thought was someone at the door and her brother had jumped out on her. As she recalled this event and allowed the panic to resurface, she asked Jesus to lift it off. As peace came upon her, she became aware in the memory that something was near her, and so she looked around and saw an angel beside her. She found new significance to Psalm 91.

When we feel lost, Jesus comes and picks us up and holds us in His arms and His light and warmth and love come and enfold us. Then we can start to believe that we're going to be all right, and as Jesus speaks to us and reveals the truth, we just know we are going to be all right. Whenever we're scared and He talks to us, we feel peace coming over our souls. When, as children, people around us hurt us and tell us that we're to blame and that we're bad, we may continue to believe this throughout life until Jesus comes and gives us understanding, showing us that He loves us and that we're special. As we release the pain and associated feelings like anger or fear to Jesus, He takes it away, and gives us His peace, setting us free. In so many different ways Jesus does meet with us and,

> *"He makes us lie down in green pastures, leading us beside quiet waters and restoring our souls."*

An alternative translation from the Hebrew is,

> *"He causes my life* (or soul, Hebrew "nephesh") *to return."*[xvii]

As God leads us into truth, He does so in a gentle, orderly way. One day as I was pondering where to start praying with a person in what seemed a whole minefield of potential exploding landmines, I heard the gentle voice say, "major on the minors" and got an impression of a bruise which was black at the centre and fading towards the edges. Then came the words, "Deal with the less painful things first and gradually the pain will lessen and then you can go to the root."

As the Holy Spirit reveals truth, He also leads us into forgiveness and, sometimes, repentance. Nearly always there is a need to forgive someone for the hurt imposed, and often there is a response that we need to repent of and receive forgiveness for. In doing so we remove the potential for satan to destroy us through exploiting ungodly attitudes such as unforgiveness, bitterness and fear. Instead, we can enjoy all the blessings of His Spirit that Jesus wants for us. Facing the hurt or pain and allowing ourselves to feel it is part of the process towards healing, as we can then release the emotions that have been buried away but which have rumbled on in a painful way influencing our present life.

Jesus always tells the truth and always wants the best for us, and so as He ministers to us it is to enable us to know the truth and to be brought to a place of peace, tranquillity and restoration,

"Jesus said, 'If you hold to my teaching, you are really my disciples. Then you will know the truth, and the truth will set you free."
John 8:31-32

His teaching includes drawing near to Him, giving Him our worries, and repenting/forgiving.[98] In coming to know the truth,

"He guides me in paths of righteousness for His Name's sake"

---

98 James 4:8, 1 Peter 5:7, Acts 3:19, Colossians 3:13.

or, as worded in the Passion Translation footnote,

"Circular paths of righteousness." Psalm 23:3

Brian Simmon[xviii] explains that,

> It is a common trait for sheep on the hillsides of Israel to circle their way up higher. They eventually form a path that keeps leading them higher. That is what David is referring to here. Each step we take following our Shepherd will lead us higher, even though we may seem to be going in circles.

So often during ministry that takes many months some have queried whether they are going around in circles. I have always been able to reassure them that even when the Spirit revisits a specific healing it is to go deeper with the healing. All ministry led by Him takes a person higher and higher in the Shepherd's presence.

As healing takes place, we walk away from emotions like fear, anger or bitterness, and walk into freedom, where peace, love and joy live in our hearts. As we continue to walk in paths of righteousness, we can choose to talk to Jesus about everything that affects us adversely and allow Him to help us in keeping free from all that would oppress us. We can choose to think with the mind of Christ, keeping our thinking Biblical and our emotions and attitudes healthy. This safeguards us from lasting effects of oppression, whether through other people, circumstances or directly from satan.

Continuing with Psalm 23:4,

> *"Even though I walk through the valley of the shadow of death, I will fear no evil for you are with me; your rod and your staff, they comfort me."*

As we walk through life, we need not fear oppression of any kind because His rod and His staff comfort us. His Spirit guides and His Son protects. And so, as we embrace the good things of Jesus, we don't need to be bound by negative emotions again for we will recognise what is happening and turn to Him. Sometimes we won't even know what is wrong, or why we're feeling as we do, but if we ask Jesus, He will show us and help us to put it right. At times when we experience stress and pressure, we can come to Him and talk it through with Him, one step at a time, describing what has happened, how we feel and what thoughts we have. As we go into a full explanation of what has happened, the negative feelings of panic, fear, or overwhelming hopelessness will surface and we can ask Jesus to take them away and give us His peace instead. In this way, we ensure that we don't allow continuing stress or pressure to build up internally with the potential of destroying us.

Jesus teaches us that He even loves those who deliberately hurt although He hates the sin. He understands why they behave as they do and wants to redeem them. When we're hurt by someone, we often want to hurt that person back, but Jesus is not like that. If He was, then we would have no hope. He truly loves us and shows us how to love. He shows love where there is hate, gives peace in place of fear, and replaces anger with kindness. In loving Jesus, we want to do what He wants us to do, but for this to take place we need His help and His grace. Living moment by moment with Him in the knowledge of His love for us gives us the security that we cannot find in the world.

What does Jesus say to us? When we're lost and frightened, He invites us to ask Him what to do and where to go. Our part is to want what Jesus wants, to walk in the paths of righteousness that He shows us. If we seek Him and His wishes, we can have confidence that we are being guided by Him. If we say we want what Jesus wants, but in our hearts want something different, then we mislead ourselves.

Jesus wants us to have a pure heart and not a divided one, a discerning ear and a responsive will. As we walk in the way of the Spirit, then God is free to bless us with the good things; with freedom, love and hope, and satan will be forced to look on and witness God's blessings poured out upon us,

> *"You prepare a table before me in the presence of my enemies. You anoint my head with oil; my cup overflows."* Psalm 23:5

God sets the boundaries beyond which satan cannot go.

As God's children, we need to want to belong to Jesus in our hearts to such an extent that we look to Him at all times. Only then can we trust Him and have confidence in Him, with the assurance that even when it's dark and something bad is happening, He is still beside us,

> *"Even though I walk through the valley of the shadow of death, I will fear no evil for you are with me; your rod and your staff, they comfort me."* Psalm 23:4

In living such a lifestyle of dependence on, and obedience to God, we will experience and be able to testify that,

> *"Goodness and love will follow us all the days of our lives, and we will dwell in the house of the Lord forever."* Psalm 23:6

Reflection
God is good all the time. God is just all the time. God is loving all the time. Let us keep our gaze upon Him, receiving His love.

Paul instructs us to build ourselves up in our most holy faith by praying in the Holy Spirit and keeping ourselves in the love of God,[99] and to protect ourselves by wearing the armour of God.[100] We shall learn later

---

99 Jude 20.
100 Ephesians 6:10-11.

that it is wise to cover the threshold of our minds at all three levels with the Blood of Jesus and to put the Cross between us and the enemy. This stops the enemy from infiltrating our thoughts in deceptive ways. Bill Johnson, in his book, "Strengthen Yourself in the Lord"[xix] writes,

> David's life shows us that the ability to strengthen and minister to ourselves is a vital skill that we must learn if we are going to develop the character to fulfil our potential as kings and priests.

As we travel down this road of inner healing, it is usually not enough merely to recall a memory, and sometimes we don't remember it anyway. Rather than using our cognitive processes, we can focus on Jesus and allow Him to reveal anything from the past that awaits resolution. This means that, rather than regressing into the past, we are moving forward step by step with Him as we release the effects of any trauma to Him and receive His peace. As an aspect of this, we need to speak truth. It is the truth that sets us free. As we acknowledge that what was done against us was sin, we do not pronounce this as judgement, but simply as truth. Frequently, it is this declaration of truth that releases us from bondage to our pain through surfacing the painful emotions. As we allow them to be taken away by Jesus it is truly amazing how free we can then feel, and how easy it is for us to forgive from our heart. Then, because we have forgiven freely, we may become aware of ungodly attitudes that we have had in relation to the trauma and so we let these leave us as we turn away from them and pray a blessing over anyone who was involved. The freedom enjoyed as a consequence causes us to sing and dance in praise and thankfulness to our Redeemer.

Here is a simple prayer which we can use on our road to inner healing:

> Lord Jesus, I ask You, by Your Spirit, to surround me with Your love and show me any situation that has brought and is bringing me pain. Please help me to be willing to face the buried memories and painful emotions so that they can be brought into Your light

and taken away. Then I ask You to fill those places with Your Holy Spirit of peace and help me to forgive from my heart. In Jesus' Name, Amen.

Prayer like this can be part of our ongoing walk with Jesus so that we remain in freedom throughout our lives. Whenever something or someone upsets us, we can deal with it in this or a similar way before it starts eating away at us. This will help us to remain in peace. If the issue doesn't resolve easily, or we recognise a pattern in our generational line that persists in our life, then perhaps we need to take a further step. We will discuss this in the second book in this series,

In summary, it is wise to remember that,[xx]

A bird is not defined by being grounded, but by its ability to fly. Remember this, humans are not defined by their limitations, but by the intentions I have for them; not by what they seem to be, but by everything it means to be created in My image.

and,

"Keep your heart with all diligence, for out of it spring the issues of life." Proverbs 4:23

Chapter 2:5

Physical Healing

"'He himself bore our sins' in his body on the cross, so that we might die to sins and live for righteousness; 'by his wounds you have been healed.'"
1 Peter 2:24

God reveals Himself as a healing God, as Yahweh Rophe, one of the eight covenant names by which God revealed His nature under the Old Covenant.[101] Our Father who loves us wants us to be whole in our bodies, minds, and spirits. He never sends sickness. Sicknesses and diseases affect our bodies because we live in, and are part of, a fallen world, and because we frequently wander away from what God teaches us that would give us life in abundance. The good news is that because Jesus took our sins and sicknesses upon Himself at the cross, we can receive healing as we trust and rest in Him.

There can be many reasons why we become sick, some of which may be unknown to us, but since there is a close connection between our spirits, souls and bodies, often what distresses one distresses all. It can be that pressures and stresses, sin, unforgiveness and wounding can lead to physical ailments.

In the gospels, whenever Jesus healed a person, He didn't demand a change of lifestyle as a prerequisite to being healed. However, after

---
101 Exodus 15:26.

healing, He entreated one person to sin no more, so sin had been an issue in their life.[102] God does not lay down rules that we must obey in order to be healed. We cannot earn our healing through our own works, perhaps trying to reason out the steps we have to take in order to be healed. Although reasoning has its place in that we can reason as to which treatment to receive, or whether we are well enough to go to work or wise to be driving, it is important that we don't develop a mindset that tries to reason out how to get healed through the ministry of the Holy Spirit. Jesus, alone, qualifies us for healing by giving us His righteousness in place of our unrighteousness. This belief rooted in our hearts frequently releases miracles of healing from within us. Sometimes our misbeliefs can cause us to become double-minded and hinder our faith for healing. James writes,

> *"But let him ask in faith, with no doubting, for he who doubts is like a wave of the sea driven and tossed by the wind. For let not that man suppose that he will receive anything from the Lord; he is a double-minded man, unstable in all his ways."* James 1:6-8

It is crucial that we establish our minds and hearts in the truth of God's Word so that this is what becomes rooted with deep certainty in our hearts.

Sometimes our bodies are sick because of some deep-seated effects from trauma and woundedness in our minds, hearts and spirits. Sometimes they are sick because of attacks from satan and his kingdom of evil. Those who suffer in these ways usually lack peace. I will discuss healing and deliverance from the effects of these in the next two books of this series but, for now, I am focusing on the healing that we can receive for our bodies when the sickness or pain is purely physical.

My introduction to praying for physical healing began with my dog, Kerry. We had just come over to Northern Ireland to live and Kerry was enjoying the sea. The trouble was that she kept getting a rash after

---

102 John 5:14.

being in the water and visits to the vet were expensive. After a few weeks of this, I was telling a friend about my predicament and she suggested praying for Kerry. I hadn't even thought of that. We prayed there and then and Kerry never had any rash after that. I was surprised and delighted. I had known about the gift of healing but wouldn't have thought of asking God to heal a dog. Some weeks later, I was in class and one of the students mentioned that she had a blinding headache. I offered to pray with her, and in nervous apprehension, asked God to remove her headache. He did so immediately. That was my first healing miracle. In church one Sunday, when about to baptise a baby, the minister explained to the congregation that the baby had a club foot and would we all pray as he baptised her. The baby's foot was healed.

As I observed and heard about amazing healings in all kinds of contexts, I became more and more interested and so attended two conferences on healing led by John Wimber[xxi] and a course that our minister led. I also joined my church's Prayer Ministry Team, a group of people who prayed with those who wanted divine healing. Over several years, I witnessed many physical healings which occurred directly through prayer, laying on of hands and anointing with oil. Gradually, involvement in prayer ministry for healing became a major part of my life and I came to an understanding that there are many ways in which God heals.

In our church, those in the Prayer Ministry Team frequently pray with people after the end of the services. Before the evening service, we would meet to pray and ask God for revelation insights that would speak into the lives of those present. As a consequence of hearing these insights read out during the service, individuals would frequently sense that God was speaking to them specifically, faith would rise within them and healing would follow. One Sunday evening while praying, one of the team members received the insight, "club foot." A Scout service was about to take place, and so many parents of the scouts and cubs who attended our church groups were present. After the service ended a mother came forward for prayer for her baby who had a club foot and was due to go into hospital for an operation. Two of the team members prayed with her and, a couple of weeks later, she contacted me to tell me that her baby's foot was healed and the operation had been cancelled. This lady was not normally in an evening service, but God knew she would be there that evening, knew her situation, and He wanted to heal her baby.

Once I tripped and fell out my back door onto paving. As I lay there feeling sore in every part of my body, I gently moved to find out how badly I had been hurt. My whole body was shaking, my face was sore from hitting the ground and my knees and elbows had suffered. As I got up, I became aware that I couldn't put any weight on one foot. I hopped back into the room and sat down and began to pray. I sat there for a long time, yielding to the ministry of the Holy Spirit. Gradually I began to feel better. Carefully, I stood up and was able to put my weight on my foot. I went to look in a mirror expecting to see great damage. There wasn't a mark on my face nor did any appear later. Except that I knew what had happened, there wasn't any evidence of the trauma that had affected my body. I praised and thanked God throughout the day and for many days following. Today, I look back in thankfulness and with confident faith.

My experiences of personal healings have not always been like this one. Sometimes God has encouraged me to use medical intervention but, always, He is the one who heals. At other times, God has healed me from a specific issue bit by bit over a lifetime as I abide in Him.[103]

Throughout this series, we are going to explore and enlarge our understanding and knowledge of God and His loving care for each person as He helps them to become more and more whole. Each life is a journey with God, our Father, and one in which we are progressively being saved into greater and greater well-being in Christ. Consequently, healing of our bodies, souls and spirits occurs many times throughout our lives.

---

103 Described in the third book of this series, The Ministry of The Father's Heart.

Through many prophetic passages in Scripture, God spoke His promise of a Messiah, the One who would bear away our sins, pains and sicknesses,

"Surely, he took up our pain and bore our suffering, yet we considered him punished by God, stricken by him, and afflicted. But he was pierced for our transgressions, he was crushed for our iniquities; the punishment that brought us peace was on him, and by his wounds we are healed." Isaiah 53:4-5

Some seven hundred years later, when John the Baptist was in prison, he sent a message to Jesus asking,

"Are you the one who is to come, or should we expect someone else?" Matthew. 11:3b

John may have been thinking,

"I saw the Spirit come on you when I baptised you but are you the one?"

Jesus' reply reminded him about what was there to be seen. Jesus was, and still is, recognised by His healing, saving and delivering presence. He told His followers that He came to,

"defeat the works of the devil." 1 John 3:8

The words of Luke 4:13, set out what this entailed by referring to another prophecy in Isaiah,

"The Spirit of the Lord is upon Me, Because He appointed Me to preach the Good News to the poor. He has sent Me to proclaim release to the captives, and recovery of sight to the blind, to set free those who are oppressed, to proclaim the favourable year of the Lord." Isaiah 61:1

Later, Paul was to write to the Galatian Church reminding them that,

"Christ redeemed us from the curse of the law by becoming a curse for us." Galatians 3:13a

And that through Christ we receive freedom,

"It is for freedom that Christ has set us free." Galatians 5:1a

This freedom refers to all the blessings that God has promised to those who are in Christ; freedom from the curses for disobedience mentioned in Deuteronomy 28:15-68. These curses include lack, diseases, sicknesses, mental torture, betrayal and oppression.

All who believe that Jesus took the full extent of their sins, sicknesses and pains on the cross and receive Him in their lives as Saviour and Lord are qualified through Him to be released from captivity and set free in whatever way they need. Healing is one aspect of this.[104] In these passages, the same Hebrew verb is used for removing sins as for healing sicknesses. We never need to question whether God wants to heal us.

Wherever Jesus preached the Gospel and healed the sick, He told His listeners,

"The Kingdom of Heaven is at hand." Luke 10:9

"The Kingdom of God is within you." Luke 17:21

This latter statement is key to our understanding of how healing can take place because it indicates that all that we need to be healed is within us. Another way of saying this is, "your healing is within you."[xxii] This is because our spirits are full of the Holy Spirit and are already healed. It is as this healing flows from our spirits to our bodies that we see it

---

104 Isaiah 53 and 1 Peter 2:24.

manifesting. Since our hearts are like the control centre to what happens in our lives, they are the link between our spirits and our bodies that allows healing to flow. This is why Jesus stressed we must believe and not doubt in our hearts.

Over time, Jesus sent out the twelve, then the seventy-two and, finally, commissioned all believers to,

"heal the sick, raise the dead, cleanse the lepers, cast out demons."
Matthew 10:8, 28:19- 20; Mark 16:15-18

To be able to receive healing for ourselves or to minister in prayer to others, we need to acknowledge that this ministry is the ministry of Jesus, and that any healing or help that comes to any of us does so because of an encounter with Jesus. It is the authority and power of Jesus impacting our lives and the lives of others that enables change. It is the Spirit of Jesus that brings about the transformation. What is so wonderful is that He invites us to participate with Him in bringing blessing to others. This is true in all sorts of ways; by listening, giving companionship, praying for, giving help, supporting, etc. Prayer Ministry gives us a focus for praying with or for people and therefore blessing them in Jesus' name. Saturating our lives with what brings health creates an environment in which the Kingdom of God can come to earth as in heaven and minister to the brokenhearted, the disillusioned, and the perpetrators of wickedness and evil. Living from this place of wholeness influences our prayers so that we pray from pure hearts and not from hearts that are vindictive, judgemental, or projecting pain. When we pray without prejudice based on experience, and choose not to lean on our own understanding but in all our ways acknowledge Him, we will be guided as we minister. Our relationship with God grows through listening with our spirits and depending on our Father to provide. This is discussed further in the following section, Conversations with God.

God is the One who heals us and He has chosen through His Son to empower us in this ministry to one another and He sends us out to fulfil it,

> *"He (Jesus) said to them (the disciples), "Go into all the world and preach the gospel to all creation. Whoever believes and is baptised will be saved, but whoever does not believe will be condemned. And these signs will accompany those who believe: In my name they will drive out demons; they will speak in new tongues; they will pick up snakes with their hands; and when they drink deadly poison, it will not hurt them at all; they will place their hands on sick people, and they will get well."* Mark 16:15-18

> *"They went out and preached that men should repent. And they were casting out many demons and were anointing with oil many sick people and healing them."* Mark 6:12-13

We can learn some lessons from observing how Jesus equipped His disciples to bring blessing in the form of healing and deliverance to others. The disciples came to know Jesus through sharing their lives with Him day in and day out. We can have a similar relationship with Jesus by living our lives conscious of His presence within and around us (abiding in Jesus and He is us) and through spending time inviting the Holy Spirit to fill us and empower us each day.

Our relationship with Jesus is important because in knowing Jesus personally, and in knowing His character, we are enabled to be confident in Him, to hear His leading and to distinguish between something that comes from Him and something that does not. Intimacy with God releases His power through us. In spending unhurried time with God, we create a haven, a place of rest away from the rush and busyness of life. As we rest in the Beloved, giving adoration, we are restored and equipped to go out in His name. In 2008, God gave me a sequence of words which can be taken as a cyclic framework within which to live:

"Believe…Behold…Bow Down…Rise up…Reach out…Rest (in Me)."

As we allow the Holy Spirit to expand our understanding through revelation, we can enter deeply into the fullness summarised in each word. Each is complete and together they offer a lifestyle. When we follow this progression and come into the place of rest in God, we are built up in our faith and once again can follow His leading into worship, revelation, and reaching out.

The disciples watched what Jesus did, how He interacted with people, what He said, and how He ministered. We can be helped to discern His leading and follow Him trustingly through their example and through the lives of the apostles. We must become less, so that Jesus becomes more in the eyes of others. Like the Holy Spirit, we point to Jesus. It is Jesus whom we thank, and it is to Him we give the glory. Although we rejoice whenever Jesus touches and heals or delivers someone, we do well to remember what Jesus told the disciples when they were rejoicing over such things,

> *"However, do not rejoice that the spirits submit to you, but rejoice that your names are written in heaven."* Luke 10:20

As we read through Luke 10, we learn how Jesus prepared His disciples before He sent them out. He breathed upon them, equipping them with His Spirit for the work of ministry. His directions were,

> *"Pray the Lord of the harvest to send out labourers into the harvest; go your way; behold I send you out as lambs among wolves; carry neither money bag, knapsack nor sandals."*

We are not to be weighed down by many things, especially by our own emotional baggage. We are not to become side-tracked but are to keep focussed on our goal,

> *"greet no-one along the road."*

We are to pray for the blessing of peace before beginning to pray for healing,

> *"but whatever house you enter, first say, 'Peace to this house.' And if the son of peace is there, your peace will rest on it; if not it will return to you."*

Once peace rests upon a person, they are more receptive to what Jesus wants to do. We remain, resting in the peace, listening to and following the lead of the Spirit as long as He is ministering to the person. We can enjoy this time of participation in what God is doing, feeding on what the Father gives us, healing the sick and telling them that the Kingdom of God is at hand.

After Jesus ascended to His Father, the disciples waited, as commanded, until the Holy Spirit came upon them in power to enable witness, healings, deliverances and miracles. Likewise, we need to wait before God to be filled afresh with His Holy Spirit before we move out in ministry of any kind. The apostle Paul makes it very clear, that it is through the empowering of the Holy Spirit that the members of Christ's body receive abilities to do and speak the healing words and works of Jesus.[105] Healing of every kind is from God, in the name of Jesus, and is accomplished by reliance upon the Holy Spirit. The disciples learned to listen and sometimes ask questions of the people for clarification. These were brief and to the point. If we need clarification when praying with others, we can do likewise, but we need to be careful that we don't encourage talk instead of power,

> *"For the kingdom of God is not a matter of talk but of power."*
> 1 Corinthians 4:20

Sometimes healing occurs purely as a sovereign act through the power of the Spirit, and sometimes it includes Spirit-inspired action on our part.

---

105 1 Corinthians 12-14.

If there seems to be a blockage, it is important that, like the disciples, we ask Jesus questions to gain further understanding how to continue. We always need to have a listening ear.

Healings don't necessarily happen because we copy or obey rules, but because we involve Jesus. As we grow in our relationship with Him, our belief and faith in all that He teaches grow in the depths of our hearts. It is this faith at a heart level that releases miracles and healings through us.

We have all been commissioned to pray for the sick. Jesus said,

> *"All authority has been given to Me in Heaven and on earth. Go therefore and make disciples of all nations, baptising them in the Name of the Father and the Son and the Holy Spirit, teaching them to observe all that I have commanded you; and, lo, I am with you always, even to the end of the age."* Matthew 28:19-20

He said to them, *"Go into all the world and preach the gospel to all creation. Whoever believes and is baptised will be saved, but whoever does not believe will be condemned. And these signs will accompany those who believe: In my name they will drive out demons; they will speak in new tongues; they will pick up snakes with their hands; and when they drink deadly poison, it will not hurt them at all; they will place their hands on sick people, and they will get well."* Mark 16:15-18

Jesus modelled the authority that He had been given and which He gives to all who are in Christ. We read how Jesus instructed His disciples,

> *"Heal the sick, raise the dead, cleanse those who have leprosy, drive out demons. Freely you have received; freely give."* Matthew 10:8

We then read they carried out these instructions by commanding healing in the name of Jesus. An example of this is when Peter and John were going to the temple one afternoon and healed a lame man at the gate. We are told that once he had got the attention of the man, Peter spoke these words of command,

"In the name of Jesus Christ of Nazareth, walk." Acts 3:6

...and then

"Taking him by the right hand, he helped him up, and instantly the man's feet and ankles became strong. He jumped to his feet and began to walk. Then he went with them into the temple courts, walking and jumping, and praising God." Acts 3:7-8

Peter understood that because Jesus had given him authority, he could heal the sick with a word of command. It is worth noting here that Peter helped the man to stand not to prove a point, but because he could see that the man was responding with heart belief and was ready to receive the miracle. This was the kind of faith that Jesus commended in the Centurion and in the woman who had been bleeding for twelve years.[106]

Sadly, there has often been misunderstanding as to how our faith helps us to receive healing and many people with deep faith have been damaged by being told that their lack of healing was because of their lack of faith. Jesus told His disciples that they needed faith as a grain of mustard seed and that's not much faith. He taught,

"Have faith in God... Truly I tell you, if anyone says to this mountain, 'Go, throw yourself into the sea', and does not doubt in their heart but believes that what they say will happen, it will be done for them." Mark 11:22-23

What we learn here is that faith is in God and not in healing, and that it is faith in the heart and not just in the head. As we listen to the Holy

---

106 Luke 7:1-10; 8:43-48.

Spirit to hear what He wants us to believe for ourselves or share with others, the words that we speak will go deep into the heart and inspire the sort of faith in God that brings healing. The gospel is a gospel of power, not of talk. It is the power of God working through the words from God that are effective, not our own well-meaning words. We may be tempted to give up praying for healing because we don't witness all that we read in Scripture, but Jesus would encourage us not to lower His Word to the level of our experience, but to believe His words and let our experience follow.

Praying for Physical Healing for Ourselves

Since we know Jesus has paid a heavy price on the cross so that we can be saved and healed, we know it is His will that we be well and strong and so we don't need to beg Him to heal us. As well as showing us in the Scriptures that He wants us healed, He teaches us how to receive healing.

Healing is received in the same way as salvation – by grace through faith. It is the Holy Spirit who convicts us of sin and our need for a Saviour, who releases faith within our hearts to believe, and who leads us into a confident knowing that we have been born again; this time into the Kingdom of God. In a similar way, as we meditate on the truths of God's Word, the Holy Spirit brings them to life in such a way that we receive them as revelation in our hearts. These truths, which have now become heart beliefs, include the promises that God has made in relation to health. What our spirits have already known now flows through into our hearts and we know that we know that what God's Word says about our healing is true. In those times where the process of healing takes longer, we may find that we have a conflict between what our five senses are telling us about symptoms and what we now believe in our hearts from God's Word. It is perfectly all right to acknowledge such symptoms to a doctor for medical purposes or to a physiotherapist or other professional who is seeking to help us, but, rather than focus on their perceived outcomes, we need to keep returning to having our focus on God and His promises and declaring them as true. Symptoms can come and go, increase and decrease, but God's Word is unchanging and God is faithful. As we consistently confess the promises, keeping our focus on the Healer, our bodies will come into line. God's truth is life-giving and so we will experience that life flowing into our physical bodies. We can also use our imagination under the guidance of God's Word to visualise what healing would look like for us. In these ways, we can continue to exercise our faith in the God who heals. This is one way in which I have been healed from health issues.

At times, I have known through the Holy Spirit that the enemy has been using tactics to put symptoms upon me, or to exaggerate symptoms or delay healing. At such times, I use the authority given to me to use Jesus' name. Jesus is victorious in heaven, on earth, and in hell, and so when I use His authority, every demon has to obey. Peter explains how he used faith in the name of Jesus to heal the lame man.[107]

Understanding what the armour of God is and how we can use it to exert our authority in Jesus' name helps us to defeat the tactics of the enemy. Clothing ourselves in the Gospel of peace involves knowing the promises and blessings that God wants us to have from His Word. The helmet of salvation over our minds is our protection, teaching us that we already have salvation, not only for eternity but also here on earth, as we use our authority in Jesus' name. Knowing what God has given us pushes out fear, including fear of death, because we realise the enemy has nothing over us. Our battle is against a liar and deceiver whose fiery darts can be extinguished through our faith in Jesus and His finished work.

Praying for Physical Healing for Others
A person who comes to us for prayer for healing may already be full of faith in Jesus and ready to receive their miracle. This may have happened privately through their own communing with God, or may have happened within a service where their faith was built up through

---

107 Acts 3:16.

worship and teaching, or through hearing a word of knowledge that witnessed with them. At such times, healing follows as we simply command or declare the truth from Scripture in the name of Jesus. Sometimes the Holy Spirit may guide us to declare specific commands in the name of Jesus. We may command issues such as sickness, joint pain, inflammation, darkness and depression to leave, and then command organs, blood vessels, nerves, ligaments, tendons, bones, cartilage, muscles to be healed or aligned as God created them. We may command fear to leave. The precise form of command prayer will be brought to mind by the Holy Spirit through our spirits. Sometimes the Spirit may lead us to anoint the person with oil or to lay hands on them for healing. In either case, we must show respect to the person by consulting them for permission to do so and, also, we must be sensitive as to where we touch a person. In this way many people have been healed during and after our church services.

Faith that acts as a conduit for healing is not a general faith but one that is specific to the person, and for specific sickness. Sometimes, people need to be helped to receive this kind of faith deep within their hearts so that healing can flow. One way in which we can do this is by building up their faith through testimony, and through the ministry of the Holy Spirit and the Word of God. Faith grows by seeing the power of God at work and so as we, and others, see God heal specific ailments, our confidence for healing of these ailments grows, and that confidence can spread over into other ones. If we continue praying with people for healing, the strong faith we have for a few things will grow into strong faith for more. Belief is a confident expectation. Faith is the currency of heaven, and unlike bank balances, increases with use. Faith can be present in any or all, in the one praying or in the one asking for prayer or coming on behalf of another. As we reflect on and meditate upon the healings that we read about in the gospels and in Acts, our faith in God for such miracles grows. As we read, we see that God never used a single method for healing, but met each person at their point of need in ways that were personal to them.

In the last section, when talking about the gifts of the Spirit, I mentioned the gift of faith. This gift is often released within both the person praying and the one being prayed for. It is given for a specific purpose at a specific time for a specific reason. Later, in the second book of this series, I will discuss the attributes of God within our spirits and how we can call upon these to help us as needed. The attribute of faith is one such.

We have mentioned that Jesus instructed His disciples to pray for peace whenever they entered a house. In a similar way, we can begin praying by asking the Holy Spirit to fill the person who is seeking healing with His peace. As His peace rests upon them and fills them (their house being their bodies, souls and spirits) they change focus from their illness onto Jesus, and become receptive to what He is offering. As we quietly observe this ministry of the Holy Spirit, we can ask Him to release healing and listen for any insight or instruction, only praying as the Spirit leads. He may bring a story of healing to mind, or a verse, or, simply, nothing. As we follow His lead, allowing Him freedom to minister in power, He will accomplish all that He wants to do. We are led by the Holy Spirit as we converse and pray and as we listen with spiritual ears to what God is saying, as well as listening to the person. We watch for spiritual signs of the Holy Spirit ministering as well as watching body language. Some such signs are glistening of the facial skin, fluttering of the eyelids, a serene expression, obvious "resting" in the Spirit, some trembling of or tingling in the body, heat in a part of the body, and an inner witness.

There are many voices seeking to be heard. When listening for the voice of the Spirit, we will discover that it becomes easier for us to discern His voice as distinct from the others (our own or satan's) as we spend more and more time in His presence. As a safeguard, we can declare our intention that our thinking submits to that of God in Jesus' name, because, *"the thoughts of the flesh are death but the thoughts of the Spirit are life and peace."* Romans 8:6

Even then, although we have prayed in this way, anything God tells us is filtered through our own imperfections and so will still need to be checked as coming from Him. In this way, we live in humility and with purity of heart before God. As Scripture tells us,

"We still prophesy in part." 1 Corinthians 13:9

and not in perfection. As we learn to follow God's leading while he is healing us and others, we will become more attuned to His voice within. The gift of discernment, along with knowledge of the Scriptures, remains essential for testing whether a message is from God or not.

As we pray for a person to be healed, our focus is on Jesus and on His love for that person, and so our hearts are filled with His compassionate love. There should never be any criticism, any judging, any rebuke of the person concerning their condition. God's grace and mercy flow when we are channels of His love and compassion, and His insight will address whatever needs His voice.

Sometimes healing occurs immediately, while at other times, the healing may manifest the following day or later. Sometimes when someone comes with an issue that they want healed, God appears to side-track because He wants to address something else first. Then once this has been done, healing will take place when we pray again.If there is an underlying spiritual or emotional cause then some other form of healing or restoration may need to take place first. Examples are repentance, forgiveness and inner healing (chapters 2.1-2.4), deliverance from evil spirits and restoration from the effects of severe trauma (books 2 and 3 in this series).

When we sense that the Holy Spirit has finished ministering, we can ask the person how they are feeling and whether they are aware of anything happening. At the very least, and this is an important sign, the person may describe having a profound sense of peace and awareness of God's presence. They may also be aware that there has been some definite, definable, change happening, such as heat moving through an injured arm or tingling in a sore toe. We can ask them a relevant question to determine whether there has been any change in how they feel (e.g., whether the pain, fear has left) or in their mobility. There may be healing taking place with no inner or outer visible proof other than a confident expectation that God has been at work. We can then use this information to guide us in further prayer, whether it be thanksgiving or an invitation to the Holy Spirit to continue ministering if this is what the person would like. God encourages persistent prayer, and as we persist, healing may come. At all times, we must be sensitive to the Holy Spirit and also to the well-being of the person. Sometimes it can take a long time for someone to be healed. Jesus told His disciples that when those that believed laid their hands on the sick, they would recover.[108] Recovery is a process. When healing takes place, there is joy in abundance.

There's a mystery to healing as not all are healed in the way that they hope. For example, Trophimus appears to have remained sick.[109] We must not feel guilty if we are sick, nor should we even hint at that for others. We live in a fallen world, and even though not all physical ailments are healed, every person who is sick and comes to Jesus for help, receives what He knows they need at the time.

108 Mark 16:18 NKJV.
109 2 Timothy 4:21.

SECTION 3

CONVERSATIONS WITH GOD

"Then summon Me and I will answer, or let Me speak and you reply to Me." Job 13:22

Chapter 3:1

Why Do We Want to Hear God Speak?

"Call to me and I will answer you and tell you great and unsearchable things you do not know." Jeremiah 33:3

Little did I know how much my life would change through calling out to God in my need for answers! He was guiding people to me for help, some of whom didn't know why their specific difficulties were so extreme, and so I began to ask God questions such as, "Lord, what happened in this person's life to cause this? In what way has it damaged them? How can they be restored?" Through listening to the answers given by the Holy Spirit, and through avidly searching the Scriptures, I, along with others, was given insights which were far beyond our experience or knowledge, and which led to the people finding freedom. I became passionate about hearing God speak,

"When your words came, I ate them; they were my joy and my heart's delight, for I bear your name, Lord God Almighty." Jeremiah 15:16

He loves to share our lives with us and to set us free. Jesus said to those Jews who believed in Him,

"When you continue to embrace all that I teach, you prove that you are my true followers. For if you embrace the truth, it will release true freedom into your lives." John 8:31-32. TPT

As I listened, I came to know God better, to live close to Him, and to discover His deep love for me and for others. In this way, my faith in God grew. As Paul wrote,

> *"faith comes from hearing ('akoé': spiritual hearing, discerning God's voice) the message, and the message is heard through the word* ('rhematos', a spoken word made by the living voice) *about Christ."* Romans 10:17

The Passion Translation (TPT) puts it this way,

> *"faith, then, is birthed in a heart that responds to God's anointed utterance of the Anointed One."* Romans 10:17

This lifestyle of having conversations with God is not only key to our understanding of how to resolve personal and individual issues, but also to help us in our intercessory prayer for people groups, nations and the world.

God has called us to be disciples of Jesus, to love Him and to love one another as Christ has loved us. The first question in the shorter catechism[110] states, "What is the chief end of man?" with corresponding response, "Man's chief end is to glorify God, and to enjoy him for ever." Once we discover the wonder and the joy of living face to face with our Father God, we never want to be without it. True worship, and enjoyment in our relationship with God, grows as we learn to communicate with Him through listening and talking. For years, this particular verse has repeatedly come to mind,

> *"It is written: 'Man shall not live on bread alone, but on every word that comes from the mouth of God."* Matthew 4:4

As we develop a lifestyle of communication with God through His Spirit, we nurture our inner man and flow with the ways of the Spirit,

---

110 The Westminster Shorter Catechism, The general Assembly of the Church of Scotland, 1648

grasping deep spiritual truths that cannot be learned. God has also told us to love our neighbours as ourselves, to partner with Him in sharing the Gospel, in healing the broken-hearted, and setting the captives free. We can only do this to the extent that we listen to His voice and follow His leading. Jesus encouraged His disciples in this when He said,

"My sheep listen to my voice; I know them, and they follow me." John 10:27

God urges us to listen to Him. He used the Hebrew word, "shema," meaning "listen," when guiding His chosen people out of slavery in Egypt and into the Promised Land to take up their inheritance.[111] Sometimes He repeated this word for emphasis: "shema, shema," meaning, "Listen closely." What exactly did His listeners understand from this? Implied in the Hebrew understanding of the word, "shema"[xxiii] was the call to focus or give attention to, and to respond or to obey. In ancient Hebrew, there is no separate word for "obey" and so obedience was inferred within the call to listen. The lack of attention paid to what they saw is recorded in the prophetic writings where God's disobedient people were told that they had ears but could not hear, and eyes but could not see.[112] They were hearing but not listening and obeying. In contrast, when Moses saw the burning bush that was not consumed, he turned aside to look further and investigate.

Paul writes to the Ephesian Church,

"I do not cease to give thanks for you, remembering you in my prayers, that the God of our Lord Jesus Christ, the Father of glory, may give you the Spirit of wisdom and of revelation in the knowledge of Him, having the eyes of your heart enlightened, that you may know what is the hope to which He has called you, what are the riches of His glorious inheritance in the saints, and what is the immeasurable

---

111 Deuteronomy 6:4.
112 Jeremiah 5:21 NKJV.

greatness of His power toward us who believe, according to the working of His great might that He worked in Christ when He raised Him from the dead and seated Him at His right hand in the heavenly places."Ephesians 1:16 ESV

The Spirit of wisdom and of revelation reveals wisdom and revelation to our spirits (God speaking) so that we can have an experiential knowledge of Jesus and be strengthened, encouraged, and enlightened.

There are many ways in which we can hear God's voice, many ways in which He speaks to us. All come through our hearts being enlightened by the Holy Spirit. When we consider different ways in which we hear what a family member, friend, or colleague is saying, we recall that it can be through verbal or non-verbal means, through action or body language. The possibilities are many and varied and may be different in each relationship. Our heavenly Father speaks to us in many such ways.

In Isaiah 32:1-4 we read,

"A King will reign with righteousness, and his princes according to justice! Each one will be a hiding place from the stormy wind and a secret shelter from the tempest. Life will flow from each one, like streams of water in the desert, like the refreshing shade of a massive rock in a weary, thirsty land. Then at last, eyes that are ready to see will finally be opened! Ears that are ready to hear will finally be opened! The hearts of those who were once hasty to form opinions will finally understand and know."

Isaiah is telling of a day when a King (Jesus) will come and rule, and when rulers under Him (His people) will speak what they see and hear from God and be as shelters from storms and streams of water in the desert places for those who are blinded and fearful. Even now, those who are in Christ and who live with Jesus as King and Lord of their lives, can receive revelation from God and be like shelters in the storm to others, who, consequently, will have their eyes and ears opened to the love of God as well.

I am reminded of a testimony in which a pastor was walking in the back streets of a city when he came across three young people sitting on some steps. Sensing that the girl might be in trouble, he went over to them, all the while listening for a prompt from God. He found himself asking the girl what she would like to do for a living. The girl answered that she didn't know, to which he responded with a word of knowledge, "You're going to be a cook!" She was surprised and wanted to know more. As they chatted, the pastor learnt she had an uncle who ran a diner and so he suggested that she phone her uncle and ask if she could work for him. The young boys with her wanted to know how the pastor had known the girl was to be a cook and so he told them about God, how much God loved them and how He wanted to help them. A year later the girl phoned to tell the pastor that her uncle had put her through catering school, bought a second diner, and put her in charge.

As I was considering what we could do to help ourselves in hearing God, three thoughts came to mind. We must:

o   be actively *aware* of His presence within us;
o   be *alert* in responding to Him;
o   understand some of the unique *abilities* given to us to
       enable us to relate to Him in dialogue.

As we become actively aware of what God is saying to us by His Holy Spirit, we become convicted by the truth and our thoughts are renewed. Then, as we stay alert in responding to Him, our lives are transformed through His abiding Spirit. In a similar way, God will guide us on our paths of service. Jesus showed us by example when He said that He only did what He saw His Father doing.[113] The Greek word translated "see" means "fully understand." When Jesus talked about only doing

---

113 John 5:19.

what His Father was doing, He was saying that He fully understood
what His Father wanted Him to do and then did it. Similarly, the Holy
Spirit opens our eyes to understand fully what our Father wants, and to
grow in that understanding as to how He helps people and transforms
circumstances. Anything we "see" with the eyes of our spirit, we fully
understand. We "get it" and it becomes transformational to our lives.
It witnesses to us deeply from our spirits and becomes settled as truth
within our inner being. Our minds are influenced and changed by such
encounters through revelation from the Word of God and through
revelation from the Spirit of God who alone knows the heart of God.[114]
Finally, we can draw upon the God-given abilities that are resident
within us, discussed in chapter 3.3.

As we spend time learning to communicate with God, we will have the
"eyes of our hearts enlightened"[115] and walk in the truths of Scripture
rather than in the traditions of man, or in the beliefs and mindsets
handed on to us. Then we will grow into Christ (think, act, look and
behave like Christ) "to the measure of the stature of the fullness of
Christ"[116] through having an experiential knowledge of Him. We will
"have the mind of Christ"[117] through the working of the Holy Spirit in
our spirits. As we decrease and He increases, His influence within us
changes our carnal thinking to spiritual. Let us now consider what is
key to our hearing God.

---

114 1 Corinthians 2:11.
115 Ephesians 1:18.
116 Ephesians 4:13.
117 1 Corinthians 16:2.

How Can We Prepare Ourselves?

"Trust in the Lord with all your heart and lean not on your own understanding; in all your ways submit to him, and he will make your paths straight." Proverbs 3:5-6

A Passion for God's Presence

Take a few moments to quieten your mind by worshipping and focussing on Jesus, and then listen to the response from your spirit as you ask Him what the word "residency" means for you at this time? When I asked this question in a seminar, I was given these responses: "to fill up with the fullness of God;" "Jesus in me;" "permanent - no flitting in and out;" "I am totally safe-me in Jesus;" "Heaven - God's kingdom - our place of residence in the kingdom of God;" "citizens of heaven above - kingdom rule;" "kingdom authority;" "kingdom values;" "kingdom privileges and rights;" "kingdom living, health, attitudes." Interestingly, I was expecting answers along the lines of Jesus living permanently within us and we in Him! Each of these responses revealed an aspect of "residency" and corresponded to what God wanted to reveal to that person at the time, highlighting that He relates to each of us in a specific way at a specific time. As we share our insights, we get a much bigger picture of what this word embraces. This is a reminder to us that in placing us within the body of Christ, we are enabled to receive a wider and deeper understanding of God and His Kingdom than we would otherwise have.

We only feel secure in God's love to the depth to which that love has been allowed to enter us. We may have all sorts of barriers to receiving unconditional love, some of which are unknown to us. We can ponder questions such as: "Do I ever doubt God's love for me? His power to heal me? His power to heal others?" "Am I convinced without doubt that nothing is too hard for Him?" "Do I believe He is always with me?" "How do I think of God and me?" "Do I experience God's love?"

Song of Songs in the Old Testament begins with the cry of one who longs for closeness to, and intimacy with, the Shepherd-King. The Shulamite longs to sense His presence, rest in it, and receive His love and the breath of His Spirit, but holds back because she feels so unworthy, so in need, and so worthless. She laments the neglect of her own vineyard while she has been busy looking after those of others. She longs to be like those who pasture their "sheep" near the Shepherd's tents, near the Shepherd Himself. The "sheep" are those she cares for and her longing is to be where He is and take her "sheep" with her into His presence. The Shepherd-King responds with words of affirmation and promises. Being in His presence leads to His beauty becoming hers and to her responding with worship. As the story unfolds, we learn that the Shepherd-King responds to her surrender by leading her through the "archway of trust" to the place of faith and settled security. He tends her inner garden, the garden of her heart. As I read this in The Passion Translation by Brian Simmons, I recalled a revelation that God had given to me some thirty years previously. I had heard God invite me with the words, "Come into the garden," and simultaneously I had seen an archway through which I could see a garden. Some years later this picture came back to me, but this time there was a lover's seat for two in the garden. It has remained vivid in my mind to this day, but it was only on reading Song of Songs again recently that I realised that that garden is the garden of my heart.

Much of it resonated with my life: always busy ministering to others' needs, and to some extent neglecting the deep need within me for unhurried time spent in God's presence, just Him and me. Intimacy,

"He-into-me-see" and "me-into-Him-see," is our pathway to a growing relationship with God. This allows God to reveal to me what He sees in my heart and what needs changing, so that barriers can come down and I am freed to enjoy Him more. And it offers me revelation of the heart of God, leading to me coming to know Him and His ways better.

The primary reason God wants us to listen to Him, is that He wants to reveal Himself to us and draw us into relationship with Him - truly believing and receiving His love deep within us so that we are unshakeable in feeling secure in Him. It would be good to pause here to ponder these things, and pray a prayer such as,

"Draw me into Your heart and lead me." Song of Songs 1:4 TPT

One night, several years ago, while I lay awake, thoughts arose from my spirit:

- o   "Power'"
- o   "Intimacy with Jesus"
- o   "Power" (accompanied by trembling)

God was showing me that intimacy with Him is what leads to His power being manifested through me. I reflected on the fact that when I was first baptised in the Holy Spirit, I was filled with God's love for people and was so excited. I wanted all the gifts of the Holy Spirit all at once! At that time, I thought this would be the all-important evidence of God's power within me. Since then, my focus has changed to one that is more in line with Scripture. My first passion is for a true, deep relationship with my heavenly Father through Jesus and in the Spirit. My second is that others may also have this close relationship. I love exercising the gifts for the building up of the body of Christ, but I now have this different perspective, that, rather than it being the goal, it has a purpose, which is to point to the all-important One, Jesus.

All true ministries begin in the place of intimacy with Jesus. When we walk in awareness of His presence and His glory, we become carriers of this glory. In being who we are in Christ, His work gets done. Many years ago, I had a vision that illustrated this, one that repeatedly comes to mind. I was observing a group of Christians and was aware that they were very busy maintaining all their church activities. A bright light shone above them. Nearby was another group, and the people in this group were needy, hopeless and in darkness, but the group in the light wasn't aware of them and kept on with their busyness. Then the scene changed. One of the Christians began to worship Jesus and look heavenward. The others began to join in one by one, until all were focussed on worshipping Jesus and their previous work forgotten. I then realised that the light over them had changed and was still bright, but was now a warmer, more mellow tone. As they worshipped, their attention was drawn towards the group in the darkness and they began to minister to them. The work of Jesus was being done.

When we are full of the Holy Spirit, He flows as living waters out from us and into the dry and parched lives of people. Last year at our Samuel Prayer Hub,[xxiv] someone received a vision about this. She saw water swirling around a person, which then flowed out and around some boulders. She understood that the boulders represented unsaved members in her family, and that the waters of the Holy Spirit were flowing from her and around them. Simultaneously, someone else received the words of a song, "No, not by might"[xxv] by songwriter and singer, Robin Mark. Reflecting on the words, we came to the line, "flow through this land, 'til every man, praises Your name once more." This confirmed our understanding of the vision. God was showing us how His Spirit flows out from each of His children to every person, gathering, community, city, and nation. It is in the presence of Jesus that we are transformed. When we are full of the Holy Spirit, the presence of God becomes one with us and everywhere we go we bring the atmosphere of heaven – we bring revival wherever we go – God's peace, His love,

His joy, His forbearance, His reconciliation, His wisdom. As we live in intimacy with God, we will have an increasing revelation of Him and His ways, and be drawn closer to Him.

Requisites for Engaging with God
I am reminded of a friend who reached out to God for help with the words, "Lord, please, help me keep my temper," to which He replied, "Why would you want to do that?" This shows the easy, friendly, joking response of a God who loves His daughter; a daughter who wanted to set her heart right. What are some of the ways in which we prepare our hearts to hear God? Recalling the full meaning of the word, "shema" we have the following thoughts: drawing close to God;[118] a hearing ear; a spiritually discerning ear;[119] a responsive life implying obedience;[120] a pure and expectant heart.[121]

Drawing Close to God
"Draw near to God and He will draw near to you." James 4:8

"You will seek Me and find Me when you seek Me with all your heart." Jeremiah 29:13

In spending unhurried time with God, we create a "haven," a "place of rest" away from the rush and busyness of life. As we "rest" in the Beloved, giving adoration, we are restored and equipped to go out in His name.

A Spiritually Discerning Ear
Jesus often said,

"He who has ears let him hear." Mark 4:9

---

118 James 4:8; Jeremiah 29:13.
119 Matthew 11:15; Revelation 2:29.
120 John 14:21,23; 15:14.
121 Psalm24:3-5.

The natural man cannot see the things of the Spirit of God for they are foolish to him. They must be spiritually discerned. That is why Jesus said,

"I tell you the truth, no-one can see the kingdom of God unless he is born again." John3:3

The things of the Spirit are perceived, examined, tested, assessed and decided upon spiritually. This is much easier when we set aside distractions, still our hearts and minds, focus on God, and wait quietly. Any human reasoning or experience must be subjected to the Word of God and to the Spirit. Any discussion can develop fruitfully as long as there is an active "listening" to discernment in our spirits. There needs to be a willingness to halt as soon as discernment raises a "stop" sign or to move forward as the discernment gives the "go ahead". It is essential to differentiate between what is coming from our flesh and what is rising from our spirits. We can pray,

"that the eyes of our hearts be enlightened." Ephesians 1:18-1

A Responsive Life, One of Obedience
Jesus had this to say,

"You are My friends if you do what I have commanded you." John15:14

"He who has My commandments and keeps them, it is he who loves Me. And he who loves Me will be loved by My Father, and I will love him and manifest Myself to him." John14:21

Following the commandments, truths and insights of Scripture and bringing ourselves into obedience and submission is key. Jesus said,

"Anyone who loves Me will obey My teaching. My Father will love them, and we will come to them and make our home (habitation) with them." John 14:23

Recall the insights given for the word "residency." It had often been pointed out that the word "I" in the middle of "obedience" is also central to the word "die," also at the heart of obedience,

"He must become greater; I must become less." John 3:30

"For none of us lives to himself alone, none of us dies to himself alone. If we live, we live to the Lord; and if we die, we die to the Lord. So, whether we live or die, we belong to the Lord." Romans 14:7-9

As we seek the truth in humility, we must be prepared to go where the Spirit leads.

A Pure and Expectant Heart

"Who may ascend the hill of the Lord? Or who may stand in His holy place?" writes the psalmist. *"He who has clean hands and a pure heart, who has not lifted up his soul to an idol or sworn deceitfully, He shall receive blessing from the Lord and righteousness from the God of his salvation."* Psalm 24:3-5

If we are to hear and see Jesus, then we need to remain humble before Jesus and pay attention to changing all impure motives and attitudes,

"Humble yourselves under the mighty hand of God." 1 Peter 5:6

If we are to continue on in our ability to hear and see Jesus, we must *"guard our hearts with all diligence"* Proverbs 4:23, and feed our minds with,

"whatever is true, whatever is noble, whatever is right, whatever is pure, whatever is lovely, whatever is admirable - if anything is excellent or praiseworthy - think about such things.......And the God of peace will be with you." Philippians 4:8

Every time we have a wrong thought, we are to capture it and dispel it in obedience to Christ.[122] We can ask God to alert us to sinful reactions, like judging, so that we can intercept them before we start to move with them. The Holy Spirit is grieved by ungodliness. He is free to work where there is holiness in our lives and in the Church. He releases His gifts within the believer for the good of the Church, His Body, to build up, empower, and equip us for witness through many and diverse ways.

Saturating our lives with what brings health creates an environment in which the Kingdom of God can come to earth as in heaven and we can minister to the lost, the broken-hearted, the disillusioned, and the perpetrators of wickedness and evil. Living from this place of wholeness influences our prayers so that we pray from pure hearts and not from hearts that are vindictive, judgemental, or projecting inner pain. Where there is no prejudice based on what we've heard or seen, and no leaning on our own understanding, but in all our ways acknowledging Him, we will be guided into truth.

The Process

As we settle down to spend time with God, we will need our Bibles together with a notebook and pen. Other reference sources, whether to be found in books or in technology, are helpful, but we must be careful that we do not substitute these for wanting to hear what God is saying to us through His Word.

We begin by eliminating all interference, whether external or internal. We can ask God to cleanse our minds, emotions, etc. and to sanctify our imaginations.[123] We can ask the Holy Spirit to fill us afresh. Being still, focussing on Jesus, worshipping Him in our hearts until we lose sight of ourselves and are lost in Him, we enter His rest. This is the setting aside of the flesh: of our own ideas and efforts; a setting aside of our own thinking (cognitive) and feelings (heart) so that we can listen to the Spirit, walk in the Spirit, live in the Spirit. The Holy Spirit is gentle,

---

122 2 Corinthians 10:5.
123 1 John 1:9; Isaiah 26:3 TPT.

never drawing attention to Himself, and therefore easily quenched. We must allow Him the freedom to move. Sometimes it takes a while before our whole heart is engaged with Him.

When we talk about feeling God's presence, we are referring to something internal – His love, peace and joy. The Kingdom of God is righteousness, joy and peace. God with us enables us to feel "right" with ourselves, with God and with others, and at peace and full of joy. So, first and foremost, we give God our full attention.

"My son. Give Me your attention. Incline your ear." Proverbs 4:20

This means that on these occasions we don't come with prayer lists, etc. We can do this, but not just yet when our priority is to know what God wants to say to us, or when we just want to enjoy companionship with Him. We come to meet with Him. We are essentially saying, "I give You all my attention. I worship You." The language God speaks is to the heart, so we position our hearts for God to speak,

"My son, give Me your heart, and let your eyes take delight in my ways." Proverbs 23:26

Once we are still and focussed on Jesus and have lost a sense of self, we are ready to receive. Prayer is me looking at God from within, with the eyes of my spirit, and God's eyes looking on me (Spirit to spirit). When our eyes meet, it is there that the Kingdom of God comes to earth. We can ask God what is on His heart, or simply rest and wait for Him to speak. We can ask questions. We can read Scripture with expectancy and meditate on it, letting it go deep into our hearts, and writing down what we think God is showing us. We may want to re-read earlier journals and re-engage some previous insight. Re-reading journals reminds us of vision, promises and affirmation, and alerts us to any repetition, thus confirming us in our ability to hear. Believing involves faith and action. As we believe that we can hear, we will respond to what we hear with faith,

"And without faith it is impossible to please God, because anyone who comes to Him must believe that He exists and that He rewards those who earnestly seek Him." Hebrews 11:6

Whenever God is giving revelation, it is wise to write it down. Frequently, as we begin writing, we may find that further words start to flow effortlessly from our spirits to our pens, and so we continue writing until this flow ceases. It is not the same as automatic writing[xxvi] but is a free flow of conversation from God our Father to us through His Spirit who is resident within our spirits. This enables us to receive the whole message without interrupting it or risking shutting down our receptivity. We can check later that what we have written is in line with Scripture and in keeping with God's character. This checking is carried out through the discernment in our spirits and through our knowledge of God's Word.

There are many Scriptures that encourage us to listen to God, and then act upon what we hear. One such suggests that we record what we are hearing from God, and even the very word "tablet" has meaning for us today!

"I will climb up to my watchtower and stand at my guard post. There, I will wait to see what the Lord says and how He will answer my complaint. Then the Lord said to me, 'Write My answer plainly on tablets, so that a runner can carry the correct message to others." Habakkuk 2:1-3

As I pondered this verse, an appropriate sequence of words came to me: record, reflect, receive, run with the revelation.

Some verses encourage us in persistence,

"Ask and it will be given to you; seek and you will find; knock and the door will be opened to you. For everyone who asks [and keeps

*on asking – this can be questions], receives; he who seeks [and keeps
on seeking – with all your heart] finds; and to him who knocks
[and keeps on knocking – perseverance] the door will be opened.
Which of you, if his son asks for bread, will give him a stone? Or if
he asks for a fish, will give him a snake? If you, then, though you are
evil, know how to give good gifts to your children, how much more
will your Father in heaven give good gifts to those who ask Him."*
Matthew 7:7-11 (Words in brackets are mine).

*"I waited and waited and waited for GOD. At last He looked;
finally, He listened. He lifted me out of the ditch, pulled me from the
deep mud. He stood me up on a solid rock to make sure I wouldn't
slip. He taught me how to sing the latest God-song, a praise song
to our God. More and more people are seeing this: they enter the
mystery, abandoning themselves to GOD.... Doing something
for you, bringing something to you-that's not what you're after.
Being religious, acting pious - that's not what you're asking for.
You've opened my ears so I can listen. So, I answered, 'I'm coming."*
Psalm 40:1-8 MSG

Yet others promise that as a consequence of such a prayer life, rivers of
the Holy Spirit will flow out from us to others,

*"Let anyone who is thirsty come to Me and drink - whoever believes
in Me - rivers of living water will flow from within them."* John 7:37

One Sunday evening before the service we sensed that God was
emphasizing the following:

1. "Be still and know that I am God"
2. "Listen"
3. "Then you will call on me and come and pray to me, and I will
    listen to you. You will seek me and find me when you seek me
    with all your heart."
4. "Dare to be a Daniel"

1. Be still and know that I am God

I thought about the importance of a worshipping heart and how various worship songs can help us to move deeper in greater intimacy with God; using songs that help to release us from burdens, sinful attitudes, and any blocks to communion with God; or songs that focus on God, on His worthiness, majesty, creativity, redeeming sacrifice, grace, mercy, compassion and faithfulness. As we enter into sensing the manifest presence of God upon us, we will find ourselves growing increasingly still until we are lost in His enveloping love. It is at this point that we move into a time of listening followed by worshipping, and yet more listening, then worshipping, etc.

2. Listen

As we sit quietly and listen, we will receive renewed or further revelation from God, about His character, His desires, or His direction for us at that time. This is a good place to begin before we make requests, whether for ourselves or for others, because we are still enough to hear what He wants us to hear. As we grasp with assurance that God really is a shelter to us in our lives, then we have confidence that He will be so for others. While praying for others, spending time worshipping and listening, we may be given words of encouragement for them. As we spend time in this way, Jesus becomes central in our everyday living and we deepen our dependency on Him. We may receive words of knowledge, or wisdom, or be given great faith. We may receive instruction to pray for healing. We may receive a message prophetically. We may be given a message in tongues along with interpretation. We are open to receiving whatever God wishes to give, and those for whom we are praying are likewise encouraged to receive from the One who restores.

3. *Then you will call on me and come and pray to me, and I will listen to you. You will seek me and find me when you seek me with all your heart.*

As well as being alert to what God wants to tell us, we can be sure that

He listens to us whenever, with sincere hearts, we search for answers from Him. As we dialogue back and forth, we can receive guidance through knowledge and understanding from Him. We may even find He is willing to adapt by taking our concerns into account. An example illustrating these is recorded in Exodus 3-4, when God called Moses to lead His people out from slavery in Egypt and into the Promised Land,

> *"Now Moses was tending the flock of Jethro his father-in-law, the priest of Midian, and he led the flock to the far side of the wilderness and came to Horeb, the mountain of God. There the angel of the Lord appeared to him in flames of fire from within a bush. Moses saw that though the bush was on fire it did not burn up. So Moses thought, "I will go over and see this strange sight - why the bush does not burn up." When the Lord saw that he had gone over to look, God called to him from within the bush, "Moses! Moses!" And Moses said, "Here I am."* Exodus 3:1-4

Then God introduces Himself, explains His concern,[124] and commissions Moses to carry out His plan for freeing His people.[125] There then follows a conversation in which God explains His strategy and the difficulty that Moses will face, and Moses makes excuses why he shouldn't be the one appointed to this task. Time after time, God reassures Moses on each of his concerns and gives him three signs with which to endorse his call.[126] Eventually, when Moses complains that he has never been eloquent[127] God begins to lose patience, but even so, He takes what Moses is saying into account and allows Moses' brother Aaron to be his mouthpiece.[128]

> *"He will speak to the people for you, and it will be as if he were your mouth and as if you were God to him."* Exodus 4:16

---

124 Exodus 3:7-9.
125 Exodus 3:10.
126 Exodus 3:11-4:1-9.
127 Exodus 4:10.
128 Exodus 4:10.

4. Dare to be a Daniel

Dare to follow Jesus wherever He leads us and in whatever He instructs us. We must not let any fear rule: fear of being ridiculed, fear of being wrong, or fear of losing our reputation. We must trust in God and follow Him. We can walk in humility and openness to God like Daniel who, when he was shown the revival of evil,[129] kept looking and looking to see the Lord's response to that evil. As He kept looking, he was shown the Ancient of Days taking His seat and One like the Son of Man coming and His kingdom being extended over the earth. We need vision from God to see how He is going to sustain lives in the midst of suffering and evil. We need His Word to sustain and comfort the weary. We need His touch to heal the sick. We need His authority to rebuke the enemy. We need Jesus. As we come to know Jesus more and more as our enlightenment, our wisdom, our revelation, we will have greater understanding of the hope of His calling and the surpassing greatness of His power as they apply to our lives.[130] In turn, we will be channels of that hope and power to others.

---

129 Daniel 7.
130 Ephesians 1:17-19a.

Chapter 3:3

How do we hear God's voice?

"And [I pray] that the eyes of your heart [the very center and core of your being] may be enlightened [flooded with light by the Holy Spirit] ...."
Ephesians 1:18

We are each made in the image of God. We are spirit with a soul, living in a body and, through faith in Jesus, have the Holy Spirit living within us.[131] Because we have the spiritual presence of God living inside us, we can be led by His Spirit from within our spirits.[132] This is a fulfilment of the prayer of Moses that all God's people would receive the Holy Spirit and prophesy.[133]

Choosing our own ways of working things out hinders us from following the lead from our spirits, which are under the guidance of the Holy Spirit. In doing things our own way, we may be following guidance from our souls or bodies which may differ from that of the Spirit within us. God's response to this is seen in Micah 6:8,

> *"Know, O people, the Lord has told you what is good, and that is what He requires of you: to do what is right, to love mercy, and to walk humbly with your God."* Micah 6:8

---

131 Romans 8:9, 11.
132 Romans 8:14.
133 Numbers 11:29.

Paul writes,

*"Therefore, brothers and sisters we have an obligation – but it is not
to the flesh, to live according to it. For if you live according to the
flesh, you will die; but if by the Spirit you put to death the misdeeds
of the body, you will live."* Romans 8:12-13

If we are to live by the Spirit, then we need to seek God's way for our
lives moment by moment and bring everything of the soul and body
under subjection to our spirit.

A Vision

One day I heard God say, "Prepare for the ground swell". I saw myself
clinging on to something that looked like a rock and finding it hard
to let go. I asked whether this rock was something that I depended on
other than Jesus. The response was, "the laws of the Medes and Persians."
I knew that this expression signifies any ruling or law that cannot be
humanly changed, and that God was showing me I had such a law at
work within me. But I also knew that if He was telling me this, then
even though I had something in my life that I couldn't change; He
could. I asked, "What law, Lord?" and heard the words, "the law of self-
preservation." I prayed, "Lord, I lay all such laws in my life at Your feet
and choose to look to You for protection." I detached myself from them
and their associated curses together with their influences and effects,
and then severed myself from each individual law and asked my Father,
in the Name of Jesus, to sever me from them and to heal me and direct
my paths (This process is explained in the second book of this series).
Because I knew that I had chosen to let go of these negative influences
that were controlling my life, the thought came, "It's like having the
feet taken from under me!" I immediately realised that this was what
God had meant when He said, "Prepare for the ground swell."

The words then came to me,

"All my springs of joy are in Him." Psalm 87:7

There is a river whose streams make glad the City of our God, the dwelling place of His Holy Habitation." Psalm 46

I felt an excitement in my spirit, anticipation of an exciting journey with God. I prayed, "Hold me and never let me go," and then heard the words, "canticles of grace." The word "canticle" means a hymn or song, typically with a Biblical text other than the Psalms and which forms part of a church service, or it can refer to the book, Song of Songs, in the Bible. I sensed this latter was what He was drawing my attention to, and somehow knew that as I read Song of Songs, I would be drawn into my Father's heart of love where there is completeness; including protection, health, love, presence, and power. His grace would once again flow through His words to bring about change within me. Then I sensed He was saying, "Forget how others teach or do things. Find a new path in Me. It is a path of exciting discovery in My world. It is heaven itself." I was reminded that the word for "stripes" in Isaiah 53:5 can be understood from the Hebrew to mean "fellowship" and that God was telling me that through fellowship with Him, I would be healed. Looking to, listening to, and learning from God meant that for me, I was to rely on and trust in God to provide all that I needed for myself and for ministry. This is what is meant by the words,

"do what is right, love mercy, and walk humbly with our God." Micah 6:8

Does this mean that we stop using our very good brains or our experiential wisdom or our perceptions and intuitions, all of which are a gift from God? Of course not! There is a place for using our senses, our cognitive thinking, and our feelings in life, but they must always be subject to what the Spirit reveals to us. In things of the Kingdom, we are encouraged throughout Scripture to seek revelation, understanding and wisdom from God by using our spiritual senses. And since we are children of the Kingdom, this means that any cognitive or experiential conclusions must be held in subjection to the spiritual. Our physical senses focus on the present, whereas our spiritual senses give insight about the past, present and future. When we walk by faith, we don't walk by our physical senses in that area.[134]

God has created us individually different, each with a unique purpose, and we won't find that specific purpose being lived out by another. Similarly, this is true for churches, cities, communities, nations. There are many passages in Scripture urging us to seek God's wisdom,

"Listen as wisdom calls out! .... Choose my instruction rather than silver, and knowledge rather than gold. For wisdom is far more valuable than rubies, nothing you desire can compare with it." Proverbs 8:1,10-11

"If you need wisdom ask our generous God and He will give it to you." James 1:5

Paul prays in this way for the Church;

"I keep asking that the God of our Lord Jesus Christ, the glorious Father, may give you the Spirit of wisdom and revelation, so that you may know Him better. I pray also that the eyes of your heart be enlightened in order that you may know the hope to which He has called you, the riches of His glorious inheritance in the Saints, and His incomparably great power for us who believe. That power is like the working of His mighty strength, which He exerted in Christ when He raised Him from the dead and seated Him at His right hand in the heavenly realms, far above all rule and authority, power and dominion, and every title that can be given, not only in the present age but also in the one to come." Ephesians 1:17

---

134 Hebrews 11.

Jesus is the source of all we need. His Spirit draws us to Him, and He points to the Father. He is our breath, our life. In Him, we live and move and have our being. He invites us to,

"remain in Me and I will remain in you." John 15:4

This is "residency." Jesus abides within us from the day we are born again. Paul reminds us,

"your body is the temple of the Holy Spirit." 1 Corinthians 6:19

Throughout our lives, God's Spirit is guiding, teaching, convicting of sin and sanctifying us as we co-operate with Him. And so, we *"are being transformed into His image with ever-increasing glory, which comes from the Lord, who is the Spirit"* 2 Corinthians 3:18. As we yield to the Spirit within, we become more and more filled with Him. Our hearts and minds become increasingly at one with Him. The Holy Spirit within us ministers to us, and we are in Jesus in the place of authority over dominions and powers,

"Seated in the heavenly realms in Christ Jesus." Ephesians 2:6

Because,

"That power is the same as the mighty strength he exerted when he raised Christ from the dead and seated him at his right hand in the heavenly realms, far above all rule and authority, power and dominion, and every name that is invoked, not only in the present age but also in the one to come. And God placed all things under his feet and appointed him to be head over everything for the church, which is his body, the fullness of him who fills everything in every way." Ephesians 1:19-23

The Spirit of God within us guides us, giving revelation, understanding and wisdom, but He also rests upon us ministering His grace, love and power as we quieten ourselves before Him and give Him freedom to instruct, touch and heal. In our spirits we are one with Him, and so we receive His revelation, understanding and wisdom, His faith, love and hope, and His companionship. Our part is to listen out for what He is showing us and to follow it through. Jesus is the "exact representation" of His Father,[135] and, in Christ Jesus, we represent Him in our love and compassion for others. As we abide in Him, even when we don't hear God speak to us, we can still be confident He is doing what He wants to do through us. In Isaiah 30, we are told that when we turn to the right or to the left, we will hear a voice behind us saying, "This is the way." If we are already on His path, we may not hear that voice of correction. We are not to strive. We are sheep!

Who are we Listening to?

Jesus taught that His people hear His voice[136] but, since we have many voices seeking our attention, we have to be able to discern His from others. We regularly hear other people's voices. Most frequently, we hear our own thoughts. We know that our common enemy, satan, is prowling around looking for someone to devour. One way in which he does this is by attempting to infiltrate our thoughts, and so thoughts that appear to be our own may have originated from an evil spirit. How this happens will be explained further in Book 2, of the series, *The Ministry of God's Heart*, but I will give guidelines here as to how we can prevent this intrusive voice from influencing us. Most importantly, God speaks to us, revealing His love by guiding us on His path, warning us of any danger, and helping us to grow into maturity as His people. In those times when we think we are hearing His voice, we need to pause and use our discernment and knowledge of Scripture to confirm or otherwise.

The Voices of Others

What others have said to us in the past may surface from our memories when we are asking God about something. We can be aware of this

---

135 Hebrews 1:3.
136 John 10:27 NKJV.

possibility and take steps to prevent it by choosing to submit all our thoughts to those of God.

Our Own Voice

So as to lessen the potential for our own thinking and emotions to interfere with hearing the voice of God, we can declare that we choose to submit these to God,

> *"The thoughts of the flesh are death but the thoughts of the spirit are life and peace."* Romans 8:6

> *"We demolish arguments and every pretension that sets itself up against the knowledge of God, and we take captive every thought in obedience to Christ."* 2 Corinthians 10:5

We can give God permission to over-ride our thoughts but, even then, whatever is affecting our hearts at the time could influence how we receive and interpret a revelation from God. So, we must check that what we think we are hearing is actually what God is saying to us. The gift of discernment of spirits, along with knowledge of the Scriptures, is essential for testing if a message is from God. We remember the importance of humility, of purity of heart, of obedience and accountability. Paul writes; *"We prophesy in part."*[137] As we learn to follow God's leading in healing our hearts, we will become more attuned to His voice within.

The Voice of Our Enemy, satan

It is important to remove any influence of satan and his evil spirits. In his first letter Peter says,

> *"Be well balanced and always alert, because your enemy, the devil, roams around incessantly, like a roaring lion looking for its prey to devour. Take a decisive stand against him and resist his every attack with strong, vigorous faith."* 1 Peter 5:8-9

---

137 1 Corinthians 13:9.

We can stop any influence from an evil spirit by obeying James' instruction,

"Submit yourselves, then, to God. Resist the devil, and he will flee from you." James 4:7

We do this by using the authority given to us by Jesus. We stop the enemy intruding into our thinking by praying a prayer like this: "In Jesus' name, I bind any evil spirit that is attempting to influence my thinking, and I command it not to communicate or interfere with me."

We can recognise the voice of the enemy because it is harsh, critical, judgemental, negative, steals our peace or causes concern or fear. It is deceptive and designed to harm. Evil satan pushes for a quick response, whereas God does not.

The Voice of God

God's words will agree with Scripture and will demonstrate His character and align with His ways,

"But the fruit of the Spirit is love, joy, peace, forbearance, kindness, goodness, faithfulness, gentleness and self-control." Galatians 5:22

His words bring life, hope, and direction. Some people may believe that it would be safer not to listen for the voice of God in case they get it wrong; but in doing so they miss out on having that intimate relationship with God and on receiving so much of what He wants to share with us. Paul writes,

"Do not quench the Spirit. Do not treat prophecies with contempt but test them all; hold on to what is good, reject every kind of evil." 1 Thessalonians 5:19

I have a mind that is logical and has been trained to solve problems through cognitive processes. This is highly useful in the sphere in which

I worked as a mathematics teacher and is useful in many life situations, but it continuously seeks to dominate even in matters of faith! As a consequence, my mind frequently battles with, and seeks priority over what I read in Scripture and know in my spirit.

Sometimes I, and others, may perceive wrongly through our physical senses. How often have we misjudged a situation when driving, or discovered that what we thought we heard someone say was different to what was actually said? Although physical senses are frequently strategically important in life, we need to subject these to any spiritual revelation that we receive from God. I clearly remember one morning when driving my car out of the gateway sensing a halt in my spirit but deciding to ignore it as it looked as though the car would pass through safely. As I passed a metal post, a bit sticking out scored a groove along the full length of my car. These very useful cognitive powers that we have can be helpful in developing further understanding of what God is telling us, but they should never take precedence over what our spirit receives. Throughout Scripture, God calls upon us to rely on Him and not on our own thinking and perceptions. As I previously wrote, "The things of the Spirit are perceived, examined, tested, assessed and decided upon in a spiritual way."

The Five Spiritual Senses
We can seek God, hear from Him, and check that what we think we are hearing is actually from Him, is in line with His character, His way of doing things, and with His Word. We may develop a fuller understanding of what God is saying as we use our powers of deduction and our knowledge from experience, but it is important that we check this new understanding with Him also through asking questions like, "Have I understood correctly, Lord? Please give me a Scripture to confirm that I am thinking in agreement with you, Lord." Even in using our skills and abilities, we can only understand His ways with His wisdom and revelation. In short, we need to be alert to, and use, the spiritual senses and the spiritual attributes that God has given to us (explained in the second book of this series). It is only as we practise using them that our

awareness of His "voice" increases. God communicates with our spirits. Our souls submit to and serve our spirits. They process the information received in our spirits and store it like a core processor. Our bodies also must submit to our spirits.

Isaiah prophesied that the Spirit would rest on Jesus.[138] He never resisted the Spirit and so the fullness of the Spirit rested upon Him at all times. When we are baptised in the Holy Spirit, He comes to rest upon us and will remain, if we don't resist Him. The Pulpit Commentary[xxvii] has this to say,

> *"The sanctifying and enlightening influences of the Holy Spirit. We can resist them or allow them to rest on us."*

This Isaiah passage continues,

> *"and he will delight in the fear of the Lord. He will not judge by what he sees with his eyes, or decide by what he hears with his ears; but with righteousness he will judge the needy, with justice he will give decisions for the poor of the earth…"* Isaiah 11:3-4a

Jesus Himself did not go by what He saw or heard with His physical senses, but looked to His Father for insight.

In Genesis 24, we can read a wonderful description of how Abraham showed his dependence on God to his servant and how this servant followed his example. Abraham had told the servant to go to the country of his relatives and find a wife for his son, Isaac. Here are some points worth considering,

o   Abraham remains obedient to an earlier direction from God – Isaac must not return to the homeland (verse 6).
o   Abraham demonstrates faith that God would guide his servant with an angel (verse 7).

---

138 Isaiah 11:2

o   The servant prayed to God that he would be successful that day (verse 12).

o   The servant thought of a plan (was the plan given to him by God?) and then submitted it to God for His approval and blessing (verse 14).

o   Events unfolded in line with the servant's plan, but he still didn't assume it was right with God. He continued watching her in silence so as to determine in his spirit if God's approval was present (verse 21). He decided it was all right and so gave gifts to Rebekah.

o   The servant learnt that Rebekah was a relative of Abraham's – confirmation that God had led him to the right person (verse 24). He worshipped God (verses 26-27).

o   He relates the background to his journey to Bethuel and Laban, and declares his confidence in the Lord before whom his master walks every day.

o   We learn that the servant's prayer was spoken in his heart (verse 50).

o   Laban and Bethuel declare their submission to the Lord in what they perceive to be a meeting orchestrated by God (verse 50).

o   The servant worshipped (verse 52).

o   The family allowed Rebekah to choose whether she would leave immediately (verse 58). Her agreement further confirmed what the servant had believed.

o   Isaac loved her (verse 67).

Notice that this servant paused to worship God after each step and confirmation. This can also be seen in the lives of the Patriarchs.

Reflection

You may like to read and ponder a few of the following passages where the spiritual senses are in evidence. For each, write down which spiritual senses are in operation (ears, eyes, smell, taste, touch/sense) and the immediate context (story, question, worship, timing etc.), and think about what have you learnt about listening to God from each?

> The call to Abraham (Genesis 12).
> God's covenant with Abraham (Genesis 15).
> A son promised to Sarah (Genesis 18).
> Abraham before Sodom and Gomorrah are destroyed (Genesis 18: 16ff).
> Abimelech's dream (Genesis 20).
> Sacrifice of Isaac (Genesis 22).
> A wife for Isaac (Genesis 24).
> Jacob's dream about the ladder (Genesis 28).
> Gideon and the "fleece" (Judges 6).
> God calls to Samuel (1 Samuel 3).
> God tells Samuel that Saul is to be king (1 Samuel 9:17).
> Elisha "sees" Elijah being taken to heaven in a whirlwind (2 Kings 2:11).
> Elisha and his servant "O, Lord, open his eyes and let him see!" (2 Kings 6:17).
> Nathan, the prophet (2 Samuel 12).
> Jesus and the Samaritan woman (John 4:10-19).
> Saul on the road to Damascus and Ananias' vision (Acts 9).
> Peter's vision and Cornelius' vision (Acts 10).
> John's visions (Book of Revelation).

The writer to the Hebrews instructs us to train our spiritual senses that we may all reach maturity,

> *"Solid food is for the mature, who by constant use have trained themselves to distinguish good from evil."* Hebrews 5:14

> *"But solid food is for the mature, whose spiritual senses perceive spiritual matters. And they have been adequately trained by what they've experienced to emerge with understanding of the difference*

between what is truly excellent and what is evil and harmful."
Hebrews 5:14 TPT

Hearing

God wants to open our ears to hear the sounds of heaven. With this spiritual sense, we are able to identify and discern the voice and sounds of God, angels, demonic spirits, and the sounds of activities in the spiritual realm. Adam heard the sound of God walking in the garden, Samuel heard someone call his name, those in the upper room heard wind at Pentecost, and shepherds heard the angels singing. God wants us to know what He is saying through what we hear, see, observe, think, feel, etc. He wants to bless us and bless others through us.

"My sheep listen to My voice; I know them, and they follow Me."
John 10:27

Our primary source is Scripture. It is essential that we make ourselves familiar with the whole of Scripture. God will often use our knowledge of Scripture to speak to us. Even when we hear in other ways, we will only be able to discern truth from deception on the basis of how well we know God, His ways, and His Word. Sometimes His voice is loud and clear,

"The voice of the Lord is over the waters, the Glory of God thunders, the Lord thunders over the mighty waters, the voice of the Lord is powerful......." Psalm 29:3-9

Sometimes His voice is a whisper,

"Then a great and powerful wind tore the mountains apart and shattered the rocks before the Lord, but the Lord was not in the wind. After the wind there was an earthquake, but the Lord was not in the earthquake. After the earthquake came a fire, but the Lord was not in the fire. And after the fire came a gentle whisper. When Elijah

heard it, he pulled his cloak over his face and went out and stood
at the mouth of the cave. Then the voice said to him, 'What are you
doing here, Elijah?" 1 Kings 19:9-13

It is important that we approach our times with God in a relaxed way, quiet and at rest within ourselves, and knowing that God will find a way of speaking to us whenever He so desires. Hearing nothing is not a failure. Sometimes God simply welcomes our company and chooses to enjoy companionable silence. If we are asking Him something, we may find the answer coming at a later time or growing within us over the ensuing days. We don't have to worry. God will speak when He is ready to. Our part is be alert to when He does, so that we don't miss out on what He's saying to us. Sometimes our question may receive an answer once it is re-phrased. Sometimes we have self-interest at the core when asking and need to submit our desires to God, emptying ourselves of them before we can readily receive. There are many ways in which we hear God's voice:

Frequently we hear from God through our spirits, the inner man. In Hebrew, the word for "heart" meaning "spirit" or "inner man" refers to a position in the belly. Our hearing may be through an inner witness while reading Scripture (a rhema Word). We may sense words, phrases, Scriptures rising from deep within our spirits into our minds. In those times, we are aware that they originate in the spirit and not in our heads. God-thoughts and words may come out of the blue, bubbling up from our spirits. (The Hebrew for the word, "prophet" means "to bubble up"). An example of this was when God told me the code for a suitcase lock. My mother had several such locks and wanted to give one to her granddaughter, but didn't know the code with which to open it. I had tried many combinations of numbers, all to no avail. While pausing for a cup of coffee, I asked the Lord if He would tell me what it was. Immediately, the correct sequence of numbers came from my spirit into my conscious thinking. At another time, on arriving home, one of my granddaughters had discovered to her great distress that she had lost her Girls Brigade badge. I offered to take the car to search for it in the grounds of the building where they had met. Once there, I put the headlights on full beam and searched at different places. No badge. I arrived back at the house disappointed for her. As I went through the door, I heard the words, "her shoe." There it was, in the toe of her shoe. Both of these examples show how easily I slip into trying to resolve issues myself with lack of success, and how much more successful and better fun it is when God is allowed to help.

Sometimes we may be aware that words seem to slide in from a source other than us. They cut across any train of thought that we are having, suddenly appearing unsolicited. When God is relaying something to me, it may begin like an intrusion, an interruption or a random thought, but then may flow. Usually, it is recognisable as not my own. Sometimes He shares a joke. An example of this was when I was driving home after praying and ministering with someone. There had been evidence of an evil spirit which had been commanded to leave. I was reflecting on this and asked God, "what was that, Lord?" I sensed His laughter and joined in as He replied, "Old Nick". Sometimes, when I waken during the night or first thing in the morning, God speaks to me in one of these ways or through pictures,

"The Sovereign Lord has given me a well-instructed tongue, to know the word that sustains the weary. He wakens me morning by morning, wakens my ear to listen like one being instructed." Isaiah 50:4

At other times a few words come that we recognise as not our own thoughts and are the beginning of a message. This may be a prophecy, and can be for encouragement for ourselves, for someone else, or for a group. As we begin to speak the words out or write them down, others flow behind them. It is important to follow this leading until we sense it cease. We must be wise in how we handle such insight, as it may not be appropriate to speak it out at the time. God will make it clear. We must always remain in submission to those in leadership.

It is only rarely that we may hear an audible voice. One time when driving I "heard" loud and clear, "Don't!"

It is helpful to write down any question that we want to ask, and then to write down the answer. Step by step we can have a dialogue with God, checking that what we think He is saying is in line with Scripture and His character and ways. We will be able to discern in our spirits whether something is truly from Him. If we are in doubt, then it is wise to lay it aside and pray that He will give it again in some other form if it is indeed from Him. As we continue the dialogue, we may want to stop to intercede, repent, forgive…. When the Holy Spirit starts to flow with words, it is good to write everything down so that the flow is not interrupted. Then, once the flow ceases, we can ask God to help us discern phrase by phrase whether it is truly from Him. We can ask, "Does this agree with Scripture?" "Is this in line with the character and ways of God?" "Does it honour Jesus as Lord?" "Does it produce the fruit of the Spirit?" "Does it edify?"

"The fruit of righteousness will be peace; the effect of righteousness will be quietness and confidence forever." Isaiah 32:17

It is also good to be accountable to others in the body of Christ.

Sometimes what we hear is not to be shared publicly, but given for insight as to how to pray.

If what we think we are hearing is contrary to Scripture, then we must reject it but not feel bad about it. The fact that we recognise it is not from God, is the consequence of the grace of God in our lives and to be celebrated. It is reality to accept that we will get things wrong at times, but being willing to make mistakes is part of our learning to distinguish between voices. These are times of growth and times when our Heavenly Father picks us up and witnesses to us that He is sovereign and will work good out of it. I believe, that as long as we are living in humility and in agreement with God's ways in so far as we can, and as long as we are willingly submitting ourselves to Him, we can have confidence that He will cover our mistakes and not allow any harm to anyone. The secret is to have a total growing dependency on God. When God becomes bigger than ourselves in our minds, then we can be at peace because we know He will help us resolve difficulties. He is Lord. He is beautiful. He is love. His kingdom is love. Everything He does is love. In Him we are love. Perfect love casts out fear. Love is stronger than death. Love prevails. As we love others, we love with His love and that will always bring healing in some form or other.

On those occasions when the answer we are seeking is not to be found in Scripture but in impressions, we can recognise the loving character of God as revealed in Scripture. Finding the unknown key code and the lost badge were examples of this. Everything God tells us reveals His kindness and desire to be involved in the details of our lives.

Sight
This spiritual sense enables us to see and discern substance, beings, and activity in the unseen dimension. When Jesus saw what the Father was doing, He knew and understood what the Father wanted. Revelation always brings understanding with the knowledge. There are many examples in Scripture of people seeing into the spiritual realm, as you will have discovered as you read the Scriptures given earlier. When God commissioned Jeremiah, He confirmed Jeremiah's ability to see what God was revealing,

"What do you see, Jeremiah?' 'I see the branch of an almond tree,' I replied." Jeremiah 1:11

To which God responded,

> *"You have seen correctly, for I am watching to see that my word is fulfilled."* Jeremiah 1:12

And later He instructed him,

> *"Get yourself ready! Stand up and say to them whatever I command you. Do not be terrified by them, or I will terrify you before them."* Jeremiah 1:17

In this short dialogue, we learn that God confirmed to Jeremiah that he was hearing Him correctly and then warned and prepared him for the reception that he would receive when he gave God's messages in the future.

On the day of Pentecost, Peter spoke to the assembled crowds quoting from the prophet Joel,

> *"In the last days, God says, I will pour out my Spirit on all people. Your sons and daughters will prophesy, your young men will see visions, your old men will dream dreams. Even on my servants, both men and women, I will pour out my Spirit in those days, and they will prophesy."* Acts 2:17-18

This applies to any of God's children. We may see pictures or get impressions with the eyes of our hearts.[139] Our physical eyes may be open or closed at the time. One time when I was praying, I saw two keys on a ring that looked as though they were tangled up in threads as though unused in a pocket. I asked God what the keys were and heard the answer, "discipline and freedom." I didn't know what to do with the information other than ask God to help me submit to being disciplined through it. I then forgot all about it. Many months later, one Sunday

---

139 Ephesians 1:18.

morning in a service, Charles McMullen, our minister, referred to a paradox mentioned by Gordon McDonald,[xxviii]

In the world, freedom is exalted as the notion that one can do anything he or she wants at any time. And yet, no one is freer than the person whose mind, body, and soul are conditioned to grow and flourish. He quotes Elton Trueblood:[xxix] "Acceptance of discipline is the price of freedom. The pole-vaulter is not free to go over the high bar except as he disciplines himself rigorously day after day. The freedom of the surgeon to use his drill, to cut away the bony structure close to a tiny nerve without severing it, arises from a similar discipline. It is doubtful if excellence in any field comes in any other way. John Milton was revealing something of his own creative power when he wrote, 'There is nothing in the world of more grave and urgent importance throughout the whole life of man than his discipline.'"

By chance, I had been reading through my records of time spent with God just prior to this and had come across my vision of the keys. Suddenly it made sense! Sometimes we only arrive at the full meaning of a vision or dream over time, so it is important to write down or make a drawing of any revelation. These records serve as enormous encouragement when read at a later date.

Sometimes impressions can be very faint. An example from ministry was the impression of a tube of toothpaste which was blocked because the toothpaste at the nozzle had dried up (no cap on). When I described it to the gentleman, he knew immediately that God was showing him that fear was blocking the flow of the Spirit out from him. Another time, while worshipping in a church, I saw a brown shoe with a couple of bands of colour, mustard and green. They were flat shoes, and someone was trying to get her foot into one of them. Later on, we were ministering in healing to the people present. A lady who could barely walk, came for prayer with the help of a friend. She told me that the doctor thought that it was the medication over the years that was causing the problem with her walking. At home she used a Zimmer, and rarely went out. I asked her if she found it difficult to get her shoe on and she said she did. Then I looked down at her feet and there were the shoes I had been shown during the service. I told her about the impression that I had received from God and she became excited at the revelation and, I believe, through that, made a connection of faith with God. Her friend and I laid hands on her feet and prayed. Two days later she was walking about unaided and driving her car. She went about giving glory to God and telling others what had happened.

While physically looking at an object in the physical realm, we may receive spiritual revelation. An example of this was when I was looking at the Nike emblem on someone's sweatshirt. God used this to show me He was pleased with the person wearing the garment. When God speaks, further investigation may yield greater understanding. For example, a picture of an armadillo led to considering the fact that an armadillo is a burrowing animal with a covering of strong, horny plates over most of its body. This understanding could lead to different conclusions, but discernment will clarify which. God may be affirming or encouraging the person to dig deeper into God and so be protected, or He may be helping the person to recognise that they have a self-made protective covering and have a propensity to hide in some way that hinders them.

We may be given an open vision, in which we can see in the spirit at the same time as seeing physically. These may synchronise and, sometimes, it can be like watching a video or scenario with the eyes of the spirit. It's a bit like a daydream and not as vivid as a trance. One evening I was worrying myself that God couldn't forgive me for something that had happened in my life many years previously. I was trying to sleep when I saw myself in an amazing scenario. In it, I was dressed in long garments and I heard God direct someone to remove the dirty clothes from me and put on priestly robes. As I watched this taking place, I heard Him tell the person to put the turban on my head. The guilt immediately left me. The following day I was at a conference with some friends and in the afternoon the speaker said that she wanted to read from Scripture, and invited us to stand. As she read the words from Zechariah 3:1-5, I was touched by God and fell to the floor. This was a rather dramatic confirmation of what I had seen the previous evening.

We may see a vision when our physical eyes are closed. This could be in a trance (a dreamlike state but awake) as with Peter on the rooftop[140] or in a dream as when Joseph was told about the coming of Jesus.[141] The times when I have had dreams have been significant in different ways. They can give revelation, direction, or warning. God often uses dreams to help a person become aware of the reason they are troubled. One dream showed me how to minister to a client. Another revealed the anxiety a friend was going through. Yet another focussed me on a way to bring unity.

I awoke from one dream with a vivid memory of the detail. It impacted me greatly and showed me how bringing two groups with opposing views, beliefs and behaviours together to work on something that focuses in some way on Jesus can lead to unity within the group. The scene began with two rival gangs rehearsing an Easter play about the crucifixion of Jesus. They had been gangs known for fighting and murder. Someone behind the scenes (I think it was a man, perhaps Jesus, but don't know as I never saw him) had managed to bring them together to work on this production. I was aware there had been trouble and difficulties, but at present they were working together as a team. I was aware that they were being impacted by the reality of the story that they were portraying to such an extent that one after the other was coming to Jesus in repentance. The scene suddenly shifted away from the performance to the mother of one of the gang members taking part in the drama. She was in a bad way herself with drugs but, because of the change in her son, had turned to Jesus and had received Him as Saviour.

140 Acts 10.
141 Matthew 1:20.

The scene then returned to the rehearsal presently going on. At some point in the dream, I learnt that the mother who had been saved had been murdered and I remember feeling so thankful that she had gone to heaven and not to hell. As the dream continued, more and more of the gang members turned to Jesus until all were saved. The person behind the scenes stayed out of the limelight but was still there, a steadying influence and respected now by each gang member. The night of the presentation arrived, and each played their part with the conviction of truth in their hearts. The effect on the audience was profound. But then, the scene shifted to the morning after the performance. I could see all the gang members from both gangs had returned to the hall where the drama had taken place the previous evening and were clearing up and cleaning it. Their lives had completely changed. I woke up.

As I reflected on this dream, I could understand how taking part in a drama about Jesus and the crucifixion could have a mighty effect on those taking part, and on those who came to see it. I'm wondering whether it would be an amazing way of helping any group of people to grow together as they grasp at a deep level the amazing gift that is offered to them in Jesus.

One Sunday evening during a service I was aware that Jesus was standing at the door of the sanctuary but, in some sense, not entering. I invited Him in, but He did not come. When I asked Him why, He responded, "It's not time yet." I understood that although He was already present in our worship that there would come a time when we would see His manifest presence in a fresh way.

When we are hearing or seeing something from God, it is beneficial to ask questions such as, "What is the purpose? Who or what does it relate to? How do I apply it?" Receive all that God gives you. It is important to record the impact, ask for explanation, confirm, remember, and recall. Revelation brings courage, confidence, faith, understanding, and knowledge.

Taste

Even as we have a physical sense that enables us to taste things in the physical realm, we also have spiritual taste buds. The spiritual world contains substances we can taste. The psalmist writes,

"Taste and see the Lord is good." Psalm 34:8

Anything that God initiates leaves us refreshed, satisfied, with a sense of well-being. Things like gossip and complaining leave a bad taste in our mouths. When we awaken our sense of spiritual taste, we are awakening our discernment of good and evil. Compare these passages,

"How sweet are your words to my taste, sweeter than honey to my mouth!" Psalm 119:103

And...

"Is there any wickedness on my lips? Can my mouth not discern malice?" Job 6:30

Meditating on the Word brings a sense of God's presence and leads us into worship.

At his initiation into his role as prophet, Ezekiel was given a scroll and instructed to eat it. It tasted like honey.[142] He was then told to speak the words that God would give him for the people. Strange encounters can happen, but the focus is not on any weirdness, but on whether there is fruit. What is God saying, instructing us in or leading us into?

Smell

There are fragrances and odours in the spiritual world, and God has created in us the ability to detect and identify them. The expression, "I smell a rat," reveals discernment. All the spiritual senses are discerners.

---

142 Ezekiel 3:1-3.

Paul writes,

"But thanks be to God, who always leads us as captives in Christ's triumphal procession and uses us to spread the aroma of the knowledge of him everywhere. For we are to God the pleasing aroma of Christ among those who are being saved and those who are perishing. To the one we are an aroma that brings death; to the other, an aroma that brings life." 2 Corinthians 2:14-16

Intimacy brings the fragrance of God and makes us carriers. When the fragrance of God comes, we know that Jesus is in the room and so we should bow in our hearts honouring the glory and presence of God amongst us. Our expression of love and worship to God brings a sweet aroma to Him and is pleasing to Him.[143]

Touch/Sense

We are able to feel and discern things spiritually with the sense of touch. Sometimes God makes His presence known in His tangible presence without words. Our hearts can be touched with empathy, by a testimony, as a result of sadness, etc.,

"Jesus was deeply moved." John 11:33

We can have heightened physical senses, e.g., in hearing birds sing. One time while speaking to my daughter on the phone, I sensed an urgency to visit a relative in hospital. I explained, rushed away, and arrived just as she died but I was able to sit with her daughter and support her.

We can bring healing to a person through touch, whether laying on of hands or something more specific. Jesus healed the blind man,[144] the leper[145] and Peter's mother-in-law through touch.[146] Many begged Him

---

143 Leviticus 1:9.
144 Mark 8:24-25.
145 Matthew 8:3.
146 Matthew 8:15.

to let them touch His cloak and be healed.[147] God cleansed Isaiah's lips[148] and strengthened Daniel.[149]

Discernment can come through any of the five spiritual senses or through unease in our spirits. In these ways, God can protect us from deception. We cannot be informed spiritually by our physical senses, but, as we live in the Spirit, with a heart of love and grace, relaxed, and with our spiritual senses alert and tuned into God, we can trust Him to give us revelation.

It is important to us to use all our spiritual senses, and, as we look to the Holy Spirit, He will teach us. They are the eyes of our heart and we can pray,

"May the eyes of our hearts be opened to receive revelation understanding of Your Kingdom ways, and may our desires become one with Yours, Lord Jesus. May we live day to day, alert to what You are showing us so that we may walk in the Spirit, live in the Spirit, and minister from the Spirit. May we decrease and You increase, so that those around us see Jesus and know they have been touched by Him. Lord, as we rest in You today, may You water our souls. In Jesus' Name. Amen."

As we receive revelation understanding, wisdom and faith from God through our spirits, we draw closer to Him, come to know Him better, and are enabled to carry His message in our hearts to others, just as Jesus did.[150] Jesus prayed,

"And this is the way to have eternal life – to know You, the only God, and Jesus Christ, the One You sent to earth.... They (My disciples) know everything I have is a gift from You for I have passed onto them the message You gave Me.... I have revealed You, Father, to them and

---

147 Matthew 14:36.
148 Isaiah 6:7.
149 Daniel 10:18.
150 John 5:38 NLT.

I will continue to do so then Your love for Me will be in them and I will be in them." John 17:3, 7-8, 26

As we interact more and more with God, we can believe and receive more and more of His love and become secure in Him. God reaches in to heal our hearts, removing fears, doubts, and unbelief. The question, "Lord, what is on Your heart today?" allows God to share with us things He is happy about and wants us to celebrate, and things that concern Him and which He wants us to pray about. We may want to ask God about how to pray for someone or something. Revelation is the explanation of God and brings insight and corresponding faith so that we can follow His direction with confidence. As well as asking for an understanding of a revelation, we can ask for wisdom in how to use it. As we hear and respond, using any insights to pray, we grow in confidence. As we sit quietly, listening and responding to God we will have revelation of the Father, and of His love for us and for others, and discern His purpose for our lives. We will be transformed to make a difference in the world around us.

Here are a few keys:

- o   Remember that God is relational and wants to spend time with us
- o   Set aside time to be alone with God, perhaps scheduling it
- o   Avoid distractions
- o   Have our Bibles, pen and paper handy so that we can write down everything we think God is telling us
- o   Be expectant. Believe that God speaks to us. Don't strive
- o   Quieten our minds. Stop analysing and attempting to solve problems, and focus on Jesus
- o   Worship
- o   Be attentive
- o   Listen. Don't talk over the Holy Spirit
- o   Ask Him about anything you need to know

God speaks in many different ways

Sometimes God speaks in a clear direct way, maybe verbally or through impressions and pictures. Many years ago, I needed to buy a car but didn't know where to go as I was new to the area at the time. I prayed, asking God, and was told the name of a garage, the make of car and even the colour. Once I got directions to the garage and asked the car salesman about buying a second-hand car, he showed me the one God had spoken to me about.

Sometimes, although clear, His response doesn't seem to make sense, or it seems irrelevant to what we are asking. At such times, it takes a large element of trust and a willingness to look foolish if we are to speak out what we think we are hearing.

In our Prayer Ministry team, we meet before the evening service to ask God for insights for people to whom He wants us to minister. Sometimes the words of knowledge are straightforward and easily recognisable as issues that God may want to alleviate; for example, heart tremor, stiff neck, skin complaint, club foot, stress because of a job situation or material witness are examples. At other times, a word of knowledge can seem rather strange and irrelevant to ministry; but strict adherence to the precise wording enables the intended recipient to recognise it as for them. Sometimes God uses this medium for reasons known only to Him. For example, on one occasion we were given the words "game, set and match," which hardly seemed like a word of knowledge for prayer for healing at the end of a service. Obedience meant that it was included. The person who responded to this had, in a previous discussion with me, said that he was sceptical about the words of knowledge that were read out during the service and yet there he was, without knowing why, sensing that these specific words were for him because he was a keen tennis player. How God loves to show people He loves them and knows all about them.

Sometimes when I have asked God to reveal His truth in a situation, it comes quickly. At other times, it comes piece by piece, here a little, there a little. At such times, it is all too easy to blame ourselves for not hearing or not having enough faith, etc. but God has a reason and patience plays its part. For example, when I felt something was wrong in a relationship but couldn't put my finger on it, I asked God about it and only received clarity over time. Each time I received an insight, my understanding as to how I was being affected by the relationship grew, until I could discern the deception which was working against me. Finally, I was shown how to pray for protection from this spirit of bewitching and manipulation.

Whenever we are ministering to others, we rely continuously on being given insights by God, which are often outside our experience or knowledge, and which are applied in faith. This leads to healing and freedom for many. Some of the ways in which God has spoken to me are:

  o   Personal revelation through Scripture; a Rhema word, that is, a Spirit-breathed word or verse.
  o   A thought rising up from my spirit, sometimes when praying, writing or speaking, sometimes after speaking in tongues.
  o   An audible voice.
  o   Tongues and Interpretation.
  o   Prophecy.
  o   Scripture reference and/or text, sometimes a character or a story in Scripture.
  o   Through an object which gives understanding.
  o   Words, both ordinary and extraordinary, e.g., "phenylketonuria" (this one came to me syllable by syllable!).
  o   Pictures.
  o   Feelings. Some feel the emotion of the person being ministered to.
  o   Nursery rhymes e.g., Humpty Dumpty, Mary, Mary Quite Contrary, Little Boy Blue. Each time, I asked God what the significance was.

o   Children's rhymes and songs, e.g., the words, "My Grandfather's Clock," may be given by God to direct us into considering the generational influences over a person's life. One time we asked in ministry where to start and were given the song, "My Bonny Lies Over The Ocean." It turned out that this person's boyfriend was in Scotland and this was what we were to talk about.

o   Dreams may be given to reveal areas that require inner healing, to give insight into ministry, help us in intercession, or instruct us in proclamation.

o   Visions. An example was a vision of people trudging through snow in Siberia. God was showing me an exodus of the Jews to their homeland. This was many years before such an exodus became widely known.

o   Hunches.

o   Through things we see around us, e.g., a bus with a poster on the side saying, "go forward together" encouraged us to do just this in ministry.

o   A thought, e.g., someone received the revelation that West Church was like a filling station where people came to be refreshed, restored, and healed, and then continue on their way.

o   Natural Realm, e.g., one day I saw a fish that had been beached and was alive, so I threw it back into the water, but it was washed ashore once again. The next time I hurled it as far as I could into the water so that the tide couldn't wash it in a second time. God spoke to me through this about the importance of not dipping in and out of a relationship with Him, but of going deep.

o   A rainbow as a symbol of hope.

o   Supernatural. Something seen in the providence of God where the impossible has happened.

o   Divine manifestations, e.g., an angel in one of the seminars, a cross shape in the sky...

God often gives insight using our own experiences and awareness of life, and He talks to us as individuals in many ways, e.g., when I saw a pattern of brain waves from an EEG (I used to know how to read these) someone else who was a nurse saw the picture of a brain. Both pointed to something wrong in the brain. Even when He gives similar pictures or dreams at different times, the interpretation will vary, so we must ask Him to make it clear.

We have thought about hearing God speak or hearing His voice and have concluded that He uses all kinds of ways in which to communicate with us, even hearing by seeing. This well-known song touches on some of that truth,[xxx]

> Red and yellow and pink and green
> purple and orange and blue
> I can sing a rainbow
> Sing a rainbow
> Sing a rainbow too
> Listen with your eyes
> Listen with your eyes and sing everything you see
> You can sing a rainbow, sing a rainbow, sing along with me

It can be a bit like listening to what we see when we are listening to God.

As I mentioned previously, God gave me a sequence of words which could be taken as a cyclic framework within which to live, a lifestyle of worship;

"Believe…Behold…Bow Down…Rise up…Reach out…Rest."

As we look behind the words, thinking about what each encapsulates, we allow the Holy Spirit to expand our thinking. Each word holds a completeness in itself and, taken together, they offer a lifestyle. When we follow this progression, coming into the place of rest in God, we are built up in our faith and once again can follow His leading back into worship, revelation, and reaching out. This brings to mind the frequency with which Abraham's servant worshipped God, returning to worship after each step on his mission.[151] Such a relationship with God develops over time. There are many different ways in which we can encourage ourselves: worship music, walks, quietness, stillness, peace, journaling, reading, praying in tongues, practising listening to our thoughts and checking whether they are from God. Time spent with God as the source of what we need, releases us to live this life in His glory and to His glory. This is His desire for each of us.

---

151 Genesis 24:10.

A Kingdom of Priests

"You are a chosen race, a royal priesthood, a holy nation, a people of God so that you would proclaim the manifestation of divine power of the One who called you out of darkness into His marvellous light." 1 Peter 2:9

When Moses ascended Mount Sinai to appear before God, he was given instructions:

"This is what you are to say to the descendants of Jacob and what you are to tell the people of Israel: 'You yourselves have seen what I did to Egypt, and how I carried you on eagles' wings and brought you to myself. Now if you obey me fully and keep My covenant, then out of all nations you will be my treasured possession. Although the whole earth is mine, you will be for me a kingdom of priests and a holy nation.' These are the words you are to speak to the Israelites." Exodus 19:3-6

In Deuteronomy we learn that three duties were expected of priests:

o   to carry the Ark of the Covenant of the Lord (presence of God) wherever they went; to stand before the Lord to minister to Him; to bless in His name (Deuteronomy 10:8-9).
o   to intercede on behalf of the people before God (Leviticus 9:22-24, Numbers 6:22-27).
o   to inquire of God for the nation (Exodus 28:30).

Peter, in his letter, reminds us that, as citizens of God's Kingdom, He has called us to be priests of God.[152] Wherever we are; we carry the presence of God, minister before Him and bless Him. In every situation, we are to intercede on behalf of people and inquire of God for them, whether as individuals or as churches or nations. Paul exhorts us to pray for everyone, especially,

> *"for kings and those in authority that we may live peaceful and quiet lives in all godliness and holiness."* 1 Timothy 2:2

He instructs us that when we don't know how to pray, the Spirit Himself will intercede,

> *"He who searches our hearts knows the mind of the Spirit, because the Spirit intercedes for God's people in accordance with the will of God."* Romans 8:26-27

He explains that because we are the temple of the Holy Spirit the Holy Spirit within guides us in our prayers.[153]

One time, while praying, I had a vision of a large hall with pillars, brightly glittering with gold. God told me that this vision was of me as His temple, the place where He resided. I was filled with His glory. Since then, I had a breath-taking revelation one morning when God made it clear to me that He calls this place within me, "The Holy of Holies." This is what Paul refers to in his letter to the Colossian Church, "Jesus in me."[154] The power of the Holy Spirit within each of us is the same power as raised Christ Jesus from the dead and is the power within us to do the works which God has prepared beforehand for us to do.[155] There is nothing that God gives us to do that is impossible for Him.

Another day I asked God to show me what it meant for me "to be in Him." Jesus said that only as we abide in Him will we bear fruit.[156] I

---

152 1 Peter 2:9.
153 1 Corinthians 3:16.
154 Colossians 1:27.
155 Ephesians 2:10.
156 John 15:4.

saw myself climbing steps and even as I was climbing, I was puzzling over why I had to climb to be with Him. In fact, I was climbing to see what it meant "to be in Him." He was seated, reigning over thrones and dominions, empires, over all creation. He was showing me that, in Christ Jesus, positionally we rule over these thrones, dominions, and all the power of the evil one, *"And God raised us up with Christ and seated us with him in the heavenly realms in Christ Jesus."* Ephesians 2:6

Seated in the heavenly places far above all principalities and powers, we are able to see things from God's perspective. Since we have been given authority in Jesus' name, at His bidding we can declare what He reveals to us as a prophetic act. In this way we trample over the works of the enemy.[157] God wants to use His people to prophesy His purposes, using His words to build up and pull down, so that His Kingdom will come in greater measure.

Over the years, God has sometimes invited me to, "come to the Mercy Seat." At first, I was unsure whether this was biblical and studied the Scriptures about the Mercy Seat. But I came to understand that this was an aspect of being seated in the heavenly places in Christ. On these occasions, it is as though I am looking down upon something that God is revealing to me while praying, or witnessing something that He wants me to know. These visits showed God's heart concerning various situations, sometimes revealing how God was seeing some conflict in the world and how He wanted us to pray with His heart, sometimes uncovering some truth that needed to be prayed about.

Portals
One time I had a vision of the temple in heaven in which I was strolling through a large entrance hall towards God. I asked what I was seeing and heard the words, "Portals of Heaven." Whereas God had shown me previously through revealing the temple within that I had been drawing Him into my heart, now He was showing me through this vision that

---

157 Luke 10:19.

He was drawing me into His heart.[158] This reminded me of a song by Paul Baloche, "I see the Lord."[xxxi]

A portal is an access point into the supernatural. Jacob experienced this.[159] There are places on earth where it is easier to access the supernatural, such as Bethel, Jerusalem and Mount Carmel in Israel, and Asuza Street, Los Angeles, where a great revival took place. They are all places where the glory of God is heavy.[xxxii] There are gatherings of people where there is an open heaven and it is easy to move supernaturally, while there are other gatherings where it seems like the heavens are as brass and it is difficult to share the Good News,

"And the heaven that is over you shall be as brass and the earth beneath like iron." Deuteronomy 28:23

There are homes where it is effortless to talk about spiritual things and pray, and there are others where it is more difficult. There are people who draw you into Jesus by their very presence, and there are others who discourage anything spiritual. Where the heavens are as brass or the earth hard, it must be ploughed through intercession, blessing and prophetically speaking the words of God. Sin will be uncovered. Territorial spirits, ruling spirits, principalities and powers must all be pulled down under the leading and revelation of the Holy Spirit through declaration.

One day while driving home after doing a prayer walk in Bangor, I heard the word, "Valkyrie" and when I researched it, I learnt that it was the spirit believed by the Vikings to determine who would live and who would die. This seemed relevant to our praying as, at one time, the Vikings had murdered many monks in a specific area of Bangor, the very area where we had been praying. This was a revelation from God about how to pray for Bangor so that the grip of death would be loosed, and people released to come to Jesus.

---

158 Song of Songs 1:4 TPT.
159 Genesis 28:16-17.

Everyone has a portal, but it can be closed, open a little, or open wide. We can prepare ourselves in whatever way God leads us to ensure that we have an open portal. Some areas or towns have a natural open heaven where worship has been to the forefront in the past and/or where God has moved powerfully, convicting many to believe and receive Jesus. Once we are experiencing an open heaven for ourselves, we are in a position to pray for heaven to be opened up over our towns. At His appointed time, God will give us the necessary revelation for such prayer,

> *"This is what the Lord says, 'Stand at the crossroads and look; ask for the ancient paths, ask where the good road is, and walk in it, and you will find rest for your souls."* Jeremiah 6:16

The ancient paths are patterns from previous times that open up the glory, and God uses these to do something fresh. There are also seasonal portals, times and seasons on the calendar where God promised to visit His people in a supernatural way, e.g., during Yom Kippur and the other feasts in the Jewish calendar.

The blood of Jesus, praise and worship, prayer, repentance and holiness, are all portals. Access through portals can allow us to see things from a heavenly perspective, as when I have been invited to the Mercy Seat to receive revelation about a place or people.[160]

Some years ago, in our church, we began a prayer group called, "Samuel Prayer Hub." We meet specifically to worship God for His own sake, and to invite Him to share with us what is on His heart. We then share any revelation that we have received to develop a fuller understanding of how God would like us to pray. One time, when a group of us was praying, we asked God how He saw the world. His response was:

---

160 Psalm 91:1.

Dog eats dog. This is what is happening in the world. Not so in My Kingdom. Light versus darkness. Shine like lights in this dark world. Radiate hope. All creation's straining to see the sons of God come into their own. Mark My words, 'less is more' in this busy world. Be still and know that I am God, God of the universe which I created with My hand and the word of My mouth. It will fade away in all its glory when I set foot on this earth. Kingdoms come and kingdoms go but My Word lasts forever. Humble yourselves under the mighty hand of God and I will bring you peace.

At another time we asked if there was portal over Bangor. The response was:

Bangor is the place of My habitation. I will not forsake it, for it is a kingdom of priests to My name. It is a Royal Borough. It is My destination. I am coming soon. My people are being prepared. Do not despise the day of small things. I am building My temple, a people of power, a holy nation, pleasing to Me. Do not grow weary or fainthearted for I will surely come. The sands of time are running out. The end is near. Watch and wait. Be ready. The time is fast approaching when I will ride in majesty into My kingdom. Pray for the good of the country. Pray for the evil minority. Pray. Pray. Pray. My kingdom is an everlasting kingdom. My righteousness exceeds all. Do not despair. Keep riding the wave of My Spirit. Keep in time and in tune. Blockages occur but I will surely come to My beloved city, the place of saints and scholars, the place of prayer and fasting, the light shining on a hill, a beacon to the nations. Tremble with fear. The time of reckoning is approaching when I will sift. Those who honour My name will see and believe.[161] Praise and worship rose, and the angels and archangels joined in. It was the valley of the angels and can be again. Take back the principal rights of the town out of

---

161 Malachi 3:16-17.

the hands of satan. Take back what belongs to you, what I gave My people. There have been marauders, vagabonds, dark powers.

At the time of receiving these words, many years ago, Bangor was referred to as a town and not a city so I pondered this. However, when I looked at the history of Bangor, I learnt that it had once been called a city and so I was satisfied that this was why God had used this word. Now, in May 2022 at the time of signing off on this book,

It has been announced that, as part of the Platinum Jubilee Civic Honours, Bangor would be granted city status by Letters Patent later in 2022.[162]

David Herzog, in his book, encourages us with these words:

The mantle over a place never dies. It is just waiting for someone with the revelation to awaken it. After God breathed on an area, a city, a ministry, or anything, it only sleeps; it never dies. Wake it up! Stir up the gifts that are in you (prophetic intercession) and stir up the mantles (like 24-hour prayer and fasting) over your region.[xxiii]

When we are praying together for others, or for some issue or group or nation, we can pray that the eyes of our hearts be opened to see revelation and have visions and that our spiritual ears be opened to hear the voice of God. We remain with each issue, one at a time, asking questions and receiving answers and discussing our insights until, collectively, we understand what God is saying, and are then able to pray in unity. We then continue the process until there is an agreed sense of completion, and move on to the next issue.

---

162 Wikipedia, Bangor, County Down

Epilogue

Our journeys throughout life are full of discoveries, each offering an opportunity for further exploration. Sometimes these discoveries are waiting to be found right where we are. In this book, *A Journey of Discovery* we have begun to explore the Kingdom of God; a Kingdom that is spiritual and not of this world, a Kingdom where love is the key, a Kingdom that will never end. We have marvelled at how much God loves each of us and found release as we have understood and applied His ways to our lives. As we continue to walk with Him and talk with Him, we grow closer to Him, enjoying ever-deepening fellowship with Him.

Many over the centuries have ventured out from their homeland, seeking lands and peoples far beyond their shores. One such explorer, Sir Francis Drake wrote a prayer as he departed from Portsmouth on the Golden Hind to raid Spanish gold on the west coast of South America.

Disturb us, Lord, when
We are too pleased with ourselves,
When our dreams have come true
Because we dreamed too little,
When we arrived safely
Because we sailed too close to the shore.
Disturb us, Lord, when
with the abundance of things we possess
We have lost our thirst
For the waters of life;
Having fallen in love with life,
We have ceased to dream of eternity
And in our efforts to build a new earth,
We have allowed our vision
Of the new Heaven to dim.

Disturb us, Lord, to dare more boldly,
To venture on wilder seas
Where storms will show Your mastery;
Where losing sight of land,
We shall find the stars.
We ask you to push back
The horizons of our hopes;
And to push back the future
In strength, courage, hope, and love.
This we ask in the name of our Captain,
Who is Jesus Christ

Perhaps you have experienced a little of the gold that God offers in His Kingdom and want to explore further. I encourage you to continue your journey of discovery. It will lead you towards a glorious future beyond this earthly life.

The Story Continues...

God gifts those who invite Jesus into their lives with the indwelling presence of His Spirit. As a consequence, we have many attributes of God within our spirits which strengthen our faith and through which we can receive insight and wisdom. We will be exploring these in the first section of Book 2 in this series.

Many of us struggle with fears, addictions and behaviours from which we seem unable to get free. Even though we may have received the fullness of the Holy Spirit and been diligent in turning away from ungodly ways and in forgiving others, perhaps receiving help through emotional healing, still we may be facing seemingly insurmountable issues in their lives. We can feel defeated while still clinging onto the God who loves us and desperately hoping for some kind of resolution. There are many reasons behind such misery, and there are also many roads to recovery, each specific to the person seeking help from God. Some of these will be explored in the second and third books in this series. In the second section of Book 2 we will discuss how we can live free from any oppression that has been directed at us by the enemy of our souls, satan. Jesus taught,

"If you hold to my teaching, you are really my disciples. Then you will know the truth, and the truth will set you free." John 8:31-32

We will be revisiting the wonderful truth that we as Christians already have the victory over evil, but that it is our responsibility to withstand any influence or oppression coming from the evil realm.

CONTACT THE AUTHOR

office@MinistryoftheFathersHeart.com

Visit our website to learn more

www.MinistryoftheFathersHeart.com

INSPIRED TO WRITE A BOOK?

Contact
Maurice Wylie Media
Your Inspirational Christian Publisher

Based in Northern Ireland and distributing around the world.
www.MauriceWylieMedia.com

Appendix

[i] Nelson Mandela 1918-2013, Portrait of An Extraordinary Man, Richard Stengel, Virgin Books, 2010.

[ii] Ministry through prayer, laying on of hands and anointing with oil.

[iii] Ministry which includes one or more from emotional healing, deliverance, fragmentation, restoration of the spirit, healing of the heart, all of which are described in the series, "The Ministry of The Father's Heart", Heather Thompson.

[iv] Seminars on Father, Son and Holy Spirit and on Baptism in the Holy Spirit.

[v] An informal group aimed at cherishing and building up women spiritually and emotionally through teaching, interaction, testimonies and some rather amateurish play-writing and acting-lots of fun!

[vi] By David L. Morris and Liz Morris, CCLI Song Number 1588843, 2000, Thankyou Music (Administered by Capitol CMG Publishing).

[vii] John Roberts | Journal-Advocate Published: September 24, 2015 at 10:12 p.m. |Updated: May 8, 2019 at 1:38a.m.

[viii] https: //en.wikipedia.org/wiki/Jackie Pullinger

[ix] George Müller (1805-1898), Christian evangelist, and founder of orphanages in England.

[x] "Turnings", Guy Chevreu, Sovereign World, Kent, England 2004, p30.

[xi] The Passion Translation, Brian Simmons.

[xii] Your Mercy lyrics © S.I.A.E. Direzione Generale, So Essential Tunes, All Essential Music, Be Essential Songs.

[xiii] Learning to Care, Selwyn Hughes and Trevor Partridge.

[xiv] Dr Albert Ellis, The ABC theory of emotions, www.positivepsychology.com/albert-ellis-abc-model-rebt-cbt. Mentioned in "Learning to Care", Selwyn Hughes and Trevor Partridge.

[xv] After God's Own Heart, Mike Bickle, Charisma House, p193.

[xvi] The Return of The Prodigal Son, Henri J. M. Nouwen, Darton, Longman & Todd.

[xvii] Brian Simmons, The Passion Translation, Psalm 23: 3 footnotes (Broad Street Publishing Group, LLC, 2018)

[xviii] Brian Simmons, The Passion Translation, Psalm 23: 3 footnotes (Broad Street Publishing Group, LLC, 2018).

[xxiv] Strengthen Yourself in the Lord, Bill Johnson, Destiny Image Publishers 2013.

[xx] Paul Young, The Shack – Reflections, 25thMarch.

[xxi] Wikipedia, John Wimber (February 25, 1934 – November 17, 1997), Pastor, California.

[xxii] Your Healing is Within You, Canon Jim Glennon, Bridge-Logos Publishing, 1980.

[xxiii] Word Study: shema – "Listen", Bible Project, YouTube, 2017.

[xxiv] A prayer gathering in which our focus is on worshipping God for Who He is, and on listening to what is on His heart for us to pray.

[xxv] From album, "Come Heal This Land: Live Worship from Northern Ireland Featuring Robin Mark", 2006

[xxvi] https: //www.britannica.com/topic/automatic-writing.

[xxvii] Delmarva Publications 2013 for Kindle.

[xxviii] Gordon McDonald, A Resilient Life, p151, (Thomas Nelson 2004).

[xxix] Elton Trueblood, The Company of the Committed (Harper Collins, 1979).

[xxx] Rainbow song, Lauryn Hill. Lyrics licensed by LyricFind.

[xxxi] I see the Lord, Paul Baloche, First Love 1998.

[xxxii] The Ancient Portals of Heaven that open up the Supernatural,

[xxxiii] The Ancient Portals of Heaven that open up the Supernatural" David Herzog.